To Caroline

In memory of our
youth and carefree
days!

Nell "Sonia"

11-2-06

The Moving Finger

by

Sonia

authorHOUSE

1663 Liberty Drive, Suite 200
Bloomington, Indiana 47403
(800) 839-8640
www.AuthorHouse.com

This book is a work of non-fiction. Unless otherwise noted, the author and the publisher make no explicit guarantees as to the accuracy of the information contained in this book and in some cases, names of people and places have been altered to protect their privacy.

© 2006 Sonia. All rights reserved.

No part of this book may be reproduced, stored in a retrieval system, or transmitted by any means without the written permission of the author.

First published by AuthorHouse 9/28/2006

ISBN: 1-4208-6135-2 (sc)
ISBN: 1-4208-6136-0 (dj)

Library of Congress Control Number: 2005905386

Printed in the United States of America
Bloomington, Indiana

This book is printed on acid-free paper.

FOR MY SONS

WILLIAM V.
THOMAS H.
JOHN C.

Acknowledgements

My husband, Paul, played a big role in bringing this book to fruition. He gave me confidence that I could succeed and encouragement to keep going. He was patient during the many months when being a writer took most of my attention and energy. And he reviewed and revised early drafts for clarity and organization.

Our good friend and neighbor Marvin Lewin gave freely of his time and computer expertise.

My old friend Anne Bippus Meek, painted the boat, with its magnificent reflections, that graces the cover of this book.

I would like to mention the invaluable gift of having Al Anon available to me when I needed it so desperately, especially my Al Anon sponsor, Barbara, who contributed more to my mental health than she will ever know.

My dear friend Jean Ringer, always accepted me, no matter what state I was in . Her friendship along with that of her husband Ted, never faltered.

The early days of our summer Bible Study group on Walloon Lake gave me friends and a purpose during some of my most unsteady times. Whatever they may have known or guessed about my depression, they made me feel welcome as we studied the words of the Bible and found hope and peace in the words of God.

Sarah Barney never gave up on me, inviting me to her wonderfully engineered parties as if there was nothing wrong with my being awkward, silent, and very, very, thin.

Preface

This is a true story. In order to ease some of the intensity certain moments have been altered slightly. Some unpleasantness has been deleted because it wasn't worthy of being mentioned. Inventing some dialogue was necessary to give clarity to the situation. Some individuals have been obscured for the sake of privacy.

The author has no intention to discredit any person for any reason. She also has no intention of being an Analyst on any level.

Table of Contents

Acknowledgements vii

Preface ix

Foreword xiii

1. A Sailing Accident 1

2. My Life Changes 5
   Surgery 5
   The Early Years 8
   After-Effects 10

3. Crises 14
   The Cuban Crisis 14
   The Way I Was 24
   City Hospital 32
   Will and Sonia 37

4. Central State Hospital 43
   I Agree to Enter Central State 43
   The First Four Weeks 45
   Conference Day 48
   The Women's Building 52
   An Incident 54
   The Canteen 57
   Addie 58
   A Short-Term Roommate 59
   The Dance 60
   A Murderess 61
   The Small Room 63
   Mary 65
   Camera Christmas 66
   The Lilly Ward 68

  A Walk to Ayres 72
  On Home Leave 75
  Press Clippings (BOX) 79

5. Attempted Suicide 80

  To My Sons 80
  The Attempt 82
  Letter from My Father 83

6. Separation and Divorce 86

  Frictions in Our Marriage 86
  Frustrations 89
  Separation 92
  Preparing for Divorce 98
  Divorce Proceedings 102

7. Back on Track 107

  Graduate School 107
  St. Anne's 112
  Public Schools 118

8. A New Life 123

  Paul and I 123
  Poems 127

9. Reflections 130

  A Meeting With Will 130
  Fear of Failure 135
  A Blanket 136
  Uncle Frank 138

Foreword

Dear Sons:

As I walked on our small island this morning at dawn, flashlight in hand, the beauty and mysteries of nature gave me great joy and peace. My mind became fixed on a project I want to finish - I am writing (rather, trying to write) a book. This project began with you alone in mind, but now I feel that it could be of interest to other people as well. It has been a daunting task for me. Although I enjoy writing, I am not an author and have minimal computer skills. I have tried to be factual, truthful, and non-judgmental.

I believe strongly that what I have to say is important to you because it will help to fill big gaps in your knowledge of what happened to me during times of your childhood and adolescence. Those were times when my mental illness and the treatments for that illness caused us to be separated, which was unfortunately for long periods of time. For complex reasons, we have avoided talking about those periods of time. However, you are grown men now. I am getting on in age (I am now in my mid-seventies), and I would like to leave you with more than my worldly possessions.

As children, did you ask where I was and when I would return? You probably got tired of asking. Maybe you learned not to ask; maybe you learned that you weren't supposed to, as if it was a forbidden secret. "Experts" say, "Wait until they ask and really want to know," but where do small children find the words to ask such questions when it all seems so painful to everyone? Maybe, since you had so many loving family members around you, it wasn't a big issue. Maybe you thought I liked the quietness of a hospital away from the toys and the noise. Maybe you thought I liked being in a place with fresh sheets, being taken care of by lovely nurses. Maybe it doesn't really matter to you now at this point in your lives. In any case, in a very short time I will turn the last page and be true to my father's philosophy of life - move on and think of happier times.

I would also like to reach out to others who are overwhelmed by life's tragedies and disappointments. Although I would not recommend the route I took through two state mental hospitals, I hope my experience will help others to work through severe traumas and intense periods of depression. I hope my experience will help people in similar situations to make a new life.

Here are just a few things I learned from my journey through mental illness: Survival skills can be acquired. Removing oneself from an unhealthy marriage can help. Returning to school at any age can be constructive. One can make do with no credit cards, bank accounts, or much self-esteem, as well as with minimum wage jobs. Suicide is not the answer.

Now that I have lived happily and healthfully for the past twenty-five years, this seems like a good time to share my thoughts and memories with you.

Love always,

Your mom

1. A Sailing Accident

Upon awakening that morning, I relished my surroundings with great tenderness and appreciation. Images of my ancestors that had lived here before me paraded through my mind. I could recall my grandmother's unique laugh with happiness.

I held on to those images as long as I could before they faded.

It was very quiet that morning except for the wind chimes on the deck, swaying gently and serenading all those who could hear them with their playful and melodic tones. Their only competition was the sound of the water at the beach, slapping the dock and boats.

The familiar and pungent scents of the old summer cottage, "Pinecrest", didn't annoy me that morning. The eight months she sat alone and closed in the North Country, among the Norway Pines, took its toll.

At age twenty-nine, I thought I had it all. My handsome and young husband, Will, whom I loved deeply, had slipped out of our love bed and was sitting on the dock. He was swishing his feet back and forth in the spring-fed water of our beloved Walloon Lake. Will was exhausted, and he desperately needed this quiet time away from the university and his law books. Our two sons were sleeping, breathing with an even rhythm. Their pink cheeks served as a reminder of the day before, when the boys had been playing on the beach and in the sun. Two-year-old Willy was walking well and entertaining us with his antics. Tom, at three months, was happy on many laps or shoulders. His large, serious, gray eyes studied us all with great anticipation as he pumped his chubby arms and legs in delight. We loved being here with my parents, and we had a whole week.

As the morning unfolded, there was no doubt about where we would spend the day. The flag on the beach had begun whipping about playfully. It would be a good day for sailing. After planning the day, Will and I decided to take Willy out with us for a short sail. Getting from the dock into the dinghy was tricky that morning. Getting out of the dinghy into the sailboat is a challenge for experienced sailors, and it was especially challenging that day for us. We all got aboard after much difficulty, and I wondered to myself why I hadn't dressed the boat earlier.

Once we were finally under sail, the sleek twenty-five foot hull and 17 square meters of sail moved us across the surface with grace and ease. The sound of the water being displaced by the gleaming mahogany-planked hull spoke to us. The mahogany had been finished "bright" this spring, and it looked magnificent in the sun.

I was the skipper and knew my boat well. I had christened her at the marina with a bottle of beer on my seventeenth birthday as my parents stood nearby. Our former boat, a Snipe, had challenged me for several years, and it had won.

It took an exceptional sailor to sail that damn boat, I often told myself, not a seasonal sailor like I was. The thousand-pound lead keel of this boat, called a "Seventeen," gave me a sense of security, even in rough seas. The mast was made of Sitka Spruce and was hollowed with a curve at the top. The first Seventeen had been built in 1934, and we had number 23.

We relaxed and enjoyed the warm sun as we glided through the third most beautiful lake in the world, according to an old *National Geographic* and hearsay. The telltale on the mast indicated a wind change, so we "came about" and headed for home.

We came about with the usual ducking, staying clear of the sails and each other. I noted the major landmarks on the way back home, two of which were the seven hills of the North Shore and the "Village." Our cottage was on the third hill and was almost lost among the Norway Pines, White Oak, and willow trees. We called it a day and decided to go in. Willy loved sailing, but he was becoming restless. Grandmother Smith would be on the beach with young Tom, waiting for our return.

We approached the dinghy that was bobbing on the sturdy buoy. The mainsail and the jib were trimmed and we were in a good position. I eased out the mainsail, and we did an easy tack around the buoy as we had done many times before. Everything seemed to be in order, but something distracted me and I felt the heavy boom hit me in the back of the head.

My head snapped back and forth once in a gentle motion. It did not feel like any damage had been done. I had no vision change or nausea. There was nothing that alarmed me or anyone else except for my father, who was sitting on the dock. He shook his head back and forth in disbelief. We were welcomed back warmly and found cold drinks in the beach house.

If I had known that day what this accident would eventually cost my family and me, I would not have been able to endure it. Weeks, months, and years of almost unbearable pain and suffering occurred as a result of this accident. Little did I know that the last normal and carefree times of my life for a very long time were ending.

2. My Life Changes

Surgery

We returned to Bloomington, Indiana, for Will's second year at Indiana University Law School. Our apartment in university housing was small but adequate for the four of us. Will and I had gone to I.U. for most of our undergraduate studies, and we loved the campus.

After about six weeks, I began to have headaches, which were unusual for me. I consulted Dr. Frank, who had delivered Tom. After seeing him several times and complaining about the headaches, he asked me to see a psychiatrist. I agreed with a laugh, as I thought that a psychiatrist presented no threat. I went to my appointment several days later.

After my appointment, the psychiatrist called Dr. Frank with the message, "She doesn't need me. She needs a neurologist." It was unbelievable to me. My only complaints were having headaches and the slight blow to the back of the head about six weeks ago. The neurologist showed Will and me an X-ray of my brain, and he pointed to a small darkened area. It was a blood clot and would have to be removed. It is hard to describe the shock that we both experienced. Dr. Frank and the neurologist agreed on a neurosurgeon. Will and I held hands as we left, encouraging each other as best we could.

The next day, I was scheduled to have brain surgery. In my organized manner, I casually wrote the date on my calendar as if it was concerning a haircut or a bridge game. As I packed, I wondered about the future of my family. Just the day before, I had gone to mass alone, praying and begging God to look over us with love and mercy. After smothering my darling boys with hugs and assurances that I would be fine and back home soon, Will and I made love and slept in each other's arms.

The doctor's office was lovely and serenely quiet. We pretended to read magazines as we waited with raw emotions. As Dr. Basil walked in, I was surprised and amused by his appearance. He was short and slight with a gray crew cut. His white tube socks were stuffed into his penny loafers. We talked over the procedure that he would follow, and he answered our pitiful questions before I was admitted to the hospital.

The next morning before the barber arrived, my mother came to my room. She clung to her composure, but her eyes were misty and her lip trembled. As we talked, she unbraided my long, shiny, chestnut-colored hair. She was remembering with agony an operation that had occurred twenty-five years earlier, during which her older daughter had died.

The barber jauntily entered the room with a flourish. He was in an absurd costume that made us smile despite our apprehensions.

"Looks like a day's work here," he joked as he lifted a handful of my heavy hair. He cut my hair in layers and stacked them neatly on the table. "Hair grows back fast - sure does," he said in a sing-song fashion. After the bulk of the hair was gone, he took out his straight razor and went over my entire head. Not a single hair could have escaped that razor.

My mother was looking at a magazine with great energy. "You look as beautiful to me now as the day you were born," she said bravely. After another embrace, she was asked to leave. Our hearts and throats ached as she turned and left.

Fortunately, I had no idea of the mental and physical scars that the operation would leave. I remember clearly being wheeled into the frigidly cold operating room. My anesthesiologist, Dr. Haswinkle, told me that I would not be totally unconscious because I would need to answer some of his questions. He explained that I would feel some sensations, but that there should be no pain. A drill was used to remove small portions of my skull to access the brain. Upon waking, my left side was paralyzed and I couldn't move my arm or leg due to swelling. I was prepared for a second surgery the next day. The swelling diminished, and I was sedated for a long time. This occurred in 1962, which was a time when medical technology was still relatively primitive compared to today.

I was a healthy, thirty-year-old woman. My life so far had been one of living in close-knit and loving family units - first with my parents and brother, and then with my husband and children. I had gone to good schools and was already well-traveled. The three school principals that I had worked for had given me glowing performance reports. Now it was time for the real test - I was going home to recuperate and care for my family. My mother went to Bloomington with us for several days, and while she cared for me, I reminisced about the early years.

The Early Years

I had a happy childhood, although I was born during a time of great sadness for my family. My sister, Lois Jane, had recently died of stomach cancer with very little warning. Her pictures at the time gave the appearance of a healthy and robust child of five. Her saucy red curls, fair skin, and reddish-brown eyes were features that she inherited from her grandmother from Tipperary, Ireland. Her twin brother from whom she had never been separated, Thomas Harvey the Fifth, had sunny blond hair and blue-gray eyes fringed with black lashes. He resembled the English side of his father's family. When Lois passed away, Tom was inconsolable. To this day, we enjoy an oil portrait of the twins that had been painted in 1930 by the Russian artist Simka Simkohovitch. He had been hired by Nell and Frank Matchette, my father's aunt and uncle.

Just before Lois died, my mother was told that she was pregnant. She often told me that I gave her the strength to go on. I was born (another blue-eyed blond) on August 18, 1931, in Long Branch, New Jersey.

We were living in New Jersey because my father worked in New York City with his uncle, Frank Matchette, as his financial advisor. He commuted daily to Manhattan by train. Uncle Frank was a wealthy hotel executive who owned apartment houses on

5th Avenue and 62nd Street. We spent many happy hours at his penthouse at 817 5th Avenue, which was where the Matchettes lived until their death.

As young children Tom and I found things to distract us when we were bored with adult conversation. Otto, the butler, amused us with stories about people who lived in the buildings and animals in the Central Park Zoo, which was just across the street. Anna, the cook, let us come into the kitchen for treats she had ready for us. Andrew, the chauffeur, was Tom's favorite. His big black car with the sliding glass window that separated him from his passengers never lost its fascination. As for me, I liked the Irish maids best. They were quick to laugh and usually found time for me. We generally found time to walk the dogs, Moo Chee and Chee Moo, in the park. Life was happy and interesting during those times of our lives. There were also the glorious times along the Jersey Shore, where we swam and explored nature's leavings.

Uncle Frank and my father had some major differences in their personalities and goals. At the age of sixteen, young Tom had come to live in New York with the Matchettes. He left his single mother and the farm in Wisconsin for an education. After graduating from Columbia, Harvard, and the London School of Economics, he wanted to be more than a family financial advisor.

With many tears, our family left New Jersey for Madison, Wisconsin, where my father became Assistant Professor of Economics while studying for a doctorate in Economics. Our lives and interests changed dramatically. Our athletic parents introduced us to winter sports with gusto. They both skied and ice skated.

Tom began playing ice hockey during grade school and became a strong, competitive skater. My joy at this time was ice boating with my father on Lake Mendota. The cold, brisk winds kept the ice smooth and polished. I sat behind my father, feeling very secure, as the sail ballooned with the north winds. The winds sent us with breakneck speed across the ice. I remember screaming with delight. The blades of the boat made a crisp rasping sound that I can still hear clearly.

Our house was small and modest on Laurence Street. My grandmother Gallagher owned the house we lived in. She was overjoyed that her son and family lived nearby. She and her second husband, A. J., lived in an old rambling house on Lake Mendota, which was within walking distance from us. Her husband was a great outdoorsman. He taught us how to recognize the tracks and scat of the wild things that lived there.

Little did I know as a young romantic girl that a neighbor on Lake Mendota would be a link to events that would affect my life profoundly for many years to come.

After-Effects

After my brain surgery, Dr. Basil told me how well I had done. He stressed that my recovery would be slow, but he explained that my body and mind would heal, even make remarkable compensations, as has indeed occurred. "Don't become pregnant for at least two years," he warned.

As I remember, the ride back to Bloomington was quiet and calm. The changes in my vision were magnified by the moving car.

Overall, I had lost half of my normal vision, and that would require a monumental adjustment. I wondered what my children would think of my bald head and the ugly scars. There was a small welcoming party for our small family which was orchestrated by my mother. It made me happy and grateful, but I wove into the bedroom feeling woozy and exhausted.

I was returning to a humming, vibrant college town bald, half blind, awkward, scared, and a candidate for seizures, all due to the recent surgery. How could I manage being a mother of two children, a wife, and a homemaker? Of course, driving was out of the question. A few weeks ago, I could do it all. My darling Will had classes to attend, assignments to do, as well as commitments to the Air Force Reserve. His income from the Reserve and a monthly check from my father paid the bills. We needed both checks.

I waited as long as I could to tell Will I was pregnant. Our youth, love, and magnetism to each other had taken their course. I knew he would be upset and blame himself, which would be totally unfair. Our mutual attraction was a gift - healthy and normal. I had been pregnant five times in the nearly six years we had been married, and two of those pregnancies had resulted in early miscarriages. After seeing Dr. Frank, I was alarmed at his concerns about this pregnancy. I assured him that being pregnant was easy for me. He set up a meeting with a psychiatrist, a neurologist, and a neonatologist. I talked to each specialist separately. The neurologist's concern was the effect that the drug Dilantin could have on a fetus, as cleft palate had been associated with this drug. The final consensus was, "If she is determined to have this child, she should do it." Another drug was substituted for Dilantin, which had been used to prevent seizures.

I'm sure the greatest burden was on Will, who was in the very difficult final year of law school. At that time, he was preparing for the final examination, which would determine whether he passed or failed. How could I explain to him how right this pregnancy was for me? In some ways, it stabilized me. An abortion was not a consideration.

Our oldest son, Willy, had started nursery school on campus. The boys and I walked to the small school every day, talking and noticing interesting things. Tom had learned to climb into his wagon by himself, for which I was grateful. I was nine months pregnant now and had slowed down, although I had taken on more responsibility in maintaining our apartment and caring for the children during the past few months. I had become more creative with scarves and hats. Although it made my sons giggle, it gave me more confidence. Will would say, "Remember only six years ago? Your sorority sent you twice to represent them in campus beauty contests." I would give him a wry and shy smile in response.

My sense of space was, and still is, a big problem. When I walked, I bumped into everything: people, doors, furniture, and anything else that was in my way. Misjudging steps was the biggest problem during this pregnancy. Each day was a challenge, and I resented being handicapped. There was no way I could live as I had earlier in my life. The notion that "nothing was impossible if one tried hard enough" did not apply in these circumstances.

The Moving Finger

Will was wonderful. He didn't complain about doing all the driving, diapers, shopping, and heavy housework, while going to classes and the library. On weekends, he also had to spend time with the Reserves.

Dr. Frank was monitoring me carefully and was pleased with how well things were going. I was scheduled to go to the same hospital, and I was given directions to follow the same routine and procedure as I had with Tom's birth. The baby clothes were fresh and ready, along with the baby equipment that we had acquired with our carefully saved S&H green stamps. Dr. Frank gave me a pat when I left his office. "See you soon! I predict this baby will arrive soon."

"I hope so," I called back, as I gingerly made my way to the waiting cab with a sense of anticipation and joy.

3. Crises

The Cuban Crisis

On a cold, gray day in October 1962 we were faced with another crisis in our young lives. I saw my handsome husband, Will, taking a short cut across the yard of the student housing. His strides were long and hurried. He had almost completed Law School. The remaining months would be challenging for Will in school and our new baby was nearly due. I was relieved that this pregnancy had gone so well despite my doctor's concerns.

As Will came closer I knew there was something wrong: the tightness in his face alarmed me.

Willy, almost four, and Tom, almost two, were all bundled up for the frosty air. Willy attended the campus preschool in the mornings, and we relished that walk together. The children were overjoyed to see their father home early. Will and I gave each other a passing hug as he entered our sparse, but adequate apartment.

"What happened", I whispered anxiously?

The Moving Finger

"We'll talk when you get back", he answered with a wink of affection.

"See you later alligators", he playfully said to our sons. The boys squealed in delight.

We walked gingerly over the patches of snow and ice looking for a treasure to take to school. Yesterday, we had found a large. black feather. These short strolls were good for me, in spite of bulky clothes and being half blind. We liked to hold hands, which made my slow, calculated steps easier.

As we entered the apartment I could hear Will talking to someone in a low voice. My mind raced with anticipation. I wanted to savor for just a few moments how well things were going for us: Will was doing well in school; my pregnancy had gone remarkably well for someone who had had major brain surgery a year earlier; the children were bright and healthy; and Will and I loved each other dearly. I told myself that I would adjust to my vision loss, and the possibility of brain seizures would surely subside in time.

Will motioned to me to sit down. As he sat next to me on our worn sofa, he said in a controlled voice: "The Air Force Reserves have been called to active duty. I am leaving for the base in Columbus early tomorrow morning; it's called the Cuban Crisis".

"All of us?", I stammered.

"Not now! he said. There are no provisions to move dependents". And this has to be kept a secret. No one can know where we are going or why."

"What about our parents?"

"Sonia, NO ONE. Do you promise?"

"I promise." I kept this promise throughout the crisis, although I was sorely tempted.

After about a week, the "Cuban Crisis" had been resolved, and with it the threat of nuclear war, but Bill's active duty Columbus command post continued. Since his reserve unit had been called up for a term of up to one year, Will took steps to bring me and the children to Columbus. He found some base housing - a one bedroom apartment in what looked like a rather seedy motel - , called his mother to come and help me for a few days with the children, and drove to Bloomington to pick me and the children up.

I have vivid memories of this move.

"I don't know how long we'll be gone, said Will, so plan accordingly. Think of absolute essentials for the three of you".

"There are four of us now, I said thoughtfully, I will take baby things too." A wave of panic pulsed through me. The color of Will's eyes had darkened as he shook his head up and down.

My mind outlined what I would need to bring: easy clothes, several books and toys, my medications and medical records, our address book and phone numbers, snacks, an easy food and drink bag, the baby's things, pen, paper, and our credit cards.

"Will, did you tell them you are in law school, that your wife is seven months pregnant, and that there are two toddlers in our family?". The impact of what was happening to us had hit. I was feeling somewhat hysterical inside. I wouldn't even be able to drive our car when we got on base - it was only yesterday that I had walked into the door again and reeled from the impact.

Keeping such accidents to myself was becoming more difficult. Makeup and ice could only do so much to conceal the bruises. It seemed as if I would never adjust to this horrible loss of vision. Spatially I was truly handicapped. "Be careful and go slowly" was always on my mind. The preoccupation with not falling or bumping into things, along with the anticonvulsant that I was taking, contributed to the dreamy state that I was in most of the time.

Will interrupted my thoughts with an answer: "Yes, I told them these things, but this is a military crisis. They are paying some of our bills, so let's pack. Leave things by the door and I'll put them in the car when it's dark".

The clothes were easy to pack. I used garbage bags for packing most things, going from room to room. Any substantial bending or lifting was left to Will. The baby was more active today than it had been, and the kicks and pokes were reassuring. It had given me great joy knowing that carrying this baby was no different than carrying the first two. I was also grateful that I had never considered terminating this pregnancy. Being told I could have other children when my health was more stable didn't interest me. I had enjoyed my first two pregnancies and had felt well and the deliveries had not been complicated. I knew this child would be healthy too. And God would surely give us strength to manage what was in store for us.

In a moment of temptation, I thought to myself that calling my parents wouldn't hurt. I reached for the phone. NO! I had promised Will and I was determined to keep my promise.

Our old banged up Ford Station Wagon was packed during that relentlessly cold night.

We left silently that morning after Will had warmed the car as much as the noisy old heater would allow him to. The boys were carried still sleeping into the car and covered with our worn comforter. On our way off campus it was surprising to see so many active people already scurrying about.

Upon our arrival at the base, we were flagged in by a bored young man, and were directed to our new temporary home The boys were wide awake by now and excited.

Will and I were determined to make this adventure as pleasant as possible for them.

Our things had been carried in and it was time to say good by. If I ever had to be an actress, it was then. "Bye, we'll be waiting for you", I said with all the calm I could muster.

His lovely dark eyes betrayed a concern beyond words, but tears did not fall. He hugged the children and said, "Be good boys and mind mommy". With as much of a grin as he could muster he said, "See you later alligators", and closed the door.

After talking briefly about Daddy and his mammoth plane, I answered as many questions as I could. "Who wants to help make peanut butter sandwiches"? We had some lunch and then decided to walk. There wasn't much to see but the air was good for us. A man was leaving the "motel", flight bag in hand. He waved to someone in the window.

Relief flooded over me- there was someone else in a similar situation. As we scrambled in from the cold I missed a small step and hit my left knee painfully against the door frame, but it protected my heavy, awkward body from falling. "Be careful and go slowly", I scolded myself. Why wasn't I learning that?

We had more sandwiches, applesauce and a cookie for dinner. We would call a cab in the morning and go to the store for milk. Small cartons of milk, a cooler, juice, bananas and fresh bread would suffice for a while. After our indoor picnic we all went into the bedroom and got into the double bed for story time and prayers. When the children dozed off I slipped out to the sofa in the other room by the door. I thought of Will preparing his very complicated and enormous plane that carried troops and even tanks for combat if necessary. He was an Air Force Commander now, a daunting task for a young man of twenty nine.

My memory of our stay on the Columbus air force base is a complete blank. Will has told me that my parents braved a bad snow storm to drive from Michigan to give me and the children support, spent some two months in a motel near the base, and helped to make Christmas a pleasant occasion, but I remember nothing of that period. I must have felt totally disoriented and subsequent events may have contributed to my amnesia.

But through this fog, I have vivid memories of the events surrounding the birth of my third son, John, on January 3rd., 1963. I cannot vouch for the accuracy of these memories, but there is no doubt as to the strength of the feelings that I experienced or the consequences that followed.

During one night (presumably that of January 2nd., I was awakened by strong contractions. I felt alone and lost. Presumably,

Sonia

Will was away on one of his many missions and my parents had left after Christmas to take care of matters in Michigan. Apparently, I had made no friends at the base, probably because of lack of any effort on my part.

I had seen a woman next door but had not met her. I knocked on her door at two AM and she peeked out of the curtain. "Oh my God", I thought, "she might not answer me". I was sweaty in the cold air.

"What d'ya want?"

"I need help. Please help me. I have a baby that wants to be born and my two small children are asleep next door".

"Oh my God, honey, you are in a mess. Are you military?

" We are now, I moaned"..

Willy was at the window, his eyes showing fear. By now, Tom was up with his foul diaper sagging. "I'll call a taxi", my neighbor called after me as I sat on the sofa hugging my children. Minutes later she reappeared saying "I'll watch your children for you". I tried to argue, replying "thanks, but they will go with me". Willy wrapped his arms around my lower legs and Tom, looking really frightened chanted "take me too, take me too" in his baby voice.

I thought my heart would break as water streamed down my legs. "Be brave my darlings, brave like Daddy. Mommy needs to go to the hospital now for the new baby, a new baby sister or brother".

The cab driver, who appeared to me as a man from heaven or my guardian angel, eased me into the back of the cab. I saw my children being ushered back into our room by the woman who had befriended me. What had I done? I reached out to them as they disappeared from view, trying to control my growing hysteria. I was whisked away to the hospital's emergency room. Hysterically I gave the people attending me my parent's Michigan phone number.

" Please call them", I begged. "My two small children are in a motel. My husband is on duty somewhere". I was panting like an animal.

A strange man in white approached me slowly as a nurse secured my feet in the stirrups." Let's have a look here," he said.

Later I awakened dazed, soaking wet. There was a terrible stench in the room. "My children, oh dear God, my children!" I moaned. Where were they? Who was with them?

Were my parents on their way? A nurse seemed to avoid me. She walked away from my bed. I forced my way out of bed and waddled painfully to the nurse's station which was close by. I demanded loudly to see my baby. "I did have a baby didn't I?" I asked weakly.

I was ushered into a wheelchair by two flustered nurses and whisked back to my room.

The Doctor I had seen before was at my bedside. "Good morning", he said cheerily, you have a strapping nine pound plus boy. You said you were going to call him "John Christian".

"Yes, but I haven't seen my baby yet", delirious with happiness at the prospect of finally seeing my son.

He came closer to the bed. His expression made my whole body freeze again.

" Baby John was taken to Children's Hospital in Indianapolis, he has a minor breathing problem." Everything went black.

Sonia

When I regained consciousness a nurse was sitting by my bed. The shades were partially closed but I could see that it was night again. The nurse offered me a pill to calm me. "No, I begged, please tell me about my children".

She took my hand and stroked it gently putting a cool cloth on my forehead. "Your husband's parents came for the two older boys as soon as they could.

They returned home after they knew you were all right: They had a young boy at home alone and they needed to return. Baby John is in the best of hands and is breathing on his own now."

"You are lying to me, he's dead, I know it", I whimpered.

"No, no, that isn't true." He is a beautiful, big baby with lots of dark hair. I know you pray because I've heard you pray for your family. Shall we pray for them all now."

"Yes, God, this is Sonia again, please take care of my precious children. They are so good and so innocent. Please personally quiet their little minds and bodies, let them know your love for them. Dear God, please watch over their Daddy. They need him and so do I. Please let us all be safely together again."

I turned my face to this thoughtful nurse as she was wiping away a tear.

" Do you think a sponge bath would feel good now?"

" Oh yes". I said gratefully.

Later I learned that when John was born he did not respond to the "birth spank".

After the spank he did not expel the fluid in his lungs. Apparently he could have drowned from this fluid.. This problem is

The Moving Finger

called "Hyline Membrane disease" and is corrected by clearing the lungs of fluid. Once this had been done, there were no detrimental effects.

Today, more than 40 years later, I can't remember what happened next. It seemed as if a large period of time is unaccounted for. " Let it go". someone said, "you have forgotten things for a good reason." I have wondered about that over the years but, who was there to ask?

We stayed in Columbus until Will was released from his active duty and returned to Bloomington when university housing became available. Will and other students who had left to serve their country had to repeat the semester of Law School that had been interrupted. John was released from the hospital, a lusty child. We packed up and returned to our small apartment and the beautiful campus.

Never was there a more joyous reunion. Will's mother and I watched with joy as Will examined his new son, happiness and relief etched on his face. Willy and Tom vied for his attention. That night, as we held each other close, we shared our trials, exhausted, but safe together.

But a return to happy days was not to be. While Will did a great deal of paper work for the University and the Air Force, I felt exhausted, often just sitting on a chair studying the floor.

There were plenty of good intentions. "Today, I'll do some cleaning. Everyone likes my meat loaf; we'll have that for dinner. But followed by "Oh Damn. Damn, Damn, we, have no tomato sauce - I don't know what we'll have". And I would dissolve into tears. But nursing and tears are not compatible, so the baby was soon hungry. "Pull yourself together," I'd scold myself. "Make breakfast, nurse John, and take out toys for Willy and Tom". One day I dissolved into tears over nothing.

Thus began a vicious circle of good intentions, fatigue and tears. After six weeks I was sleeping only four or five hours a night, had lost 15 pounds, and had become almost non-functional.

Dr. Frank was alarmed during a visit, six weeks after John's birth. "I would like you to see the psychiatrist again, Nell".

"What? Why?" I protested in frustration, my eyes beginning to well with tears.

"Jane will make an appointment for you, this is the thing to do", he said gently but firmly. Several days later I saw the same Psychiatrist I had consulted about my last pregnancy. "You are experiencing Post partum Depression, which isn't that unusual", he said. "The recent neurosurgery, the war crisis, and birth complications have been very stressful for you. It is my best judgment that you should have medical treatment in a short-term psychiatric hospital in Indianapolis".

My world was crashing again.

The Way I Was

Until these crises, fear and indecision were simply not a part of my life. I had been confident, optimistic, and active. I knew who I was. Within limits, I willingly explored new places and relationships and pursued my goals, sometimes even against parental advice.

My high school experience was enviable. I had a good blend of friends, social activities, generally good teachers, and a loving family. There was no anxiety about being sexually active, as my girlfriends and I just weren't "those kind of girls." We smoked secretly sometimes and did not drink alcohol, except at the "notorious" New Year's Eve parties we had in each other's homes. The real intent of the parties was to have the boys arrive for midnight kisses, and they came by the carloads. Unfortunately, I was not a really serious student, although my grades were quite good.

It was time to choose a college. Uncle Frank had left $4,000 each to my brother and me for our college education. In those days, that's all it took to pay for the four years. I would have liked to attend Smith, but my grades were not good enough. A friend of my mother's had gone to a Catholic women's college in Washington, D.C., called Trinity College. Trinity had a good reputation, and it was located near Catholic University and was about two miles from the White House. I was favorably impressed from what I read and heard about it.

Being a brave soul and unafraid of new ventures, I was on my way, although I had never been to Washington and knew no one there. My mother and I enjoyed the process of selecting what I would take with me. My parents drove me to the train station in Indianapolis. We had a teary farewell. As the train began to leave the station, I saw my father hand some money to the porter so he would keep an eye out for me. I was very excited about leaving home and looked forward to this change in my life.

Sonia

I met a girl named Gretchen from Batesville, Indiana, who was also on her way to Washington. She was a junior at Trinity. I learned that we were the only girls from Indiana that attended the college. As we neared the station, I was thrilled to catch a glimpse of the While House. Washington was indeed a large, very busy city where everyone seemed to be in a rush. The cab driver pointed out some landmarks as we whizzed past them. Finally, we drove through a circular drive into the lovely grounds of the campus. There were lots of young men milling around. I learned that they were from Georgetown University and had come to welcome back old friends, as well as to eye the new freshman crop. I was a bit irritated to find out that several states, including Indiana, were the butt of jokes. I had to assure other students that we lived pretty much like they did, with stores and everything.

Washington was an exciting place to live. There was much to see and do, and several people were ready and willing to show me around. We signed "in" and "out" on a ledger when we left the campus, leaving no doubts about where we were. I was not putting in a lot of time studying, and as a result, my grades began to slip. It was not helpful that during the first two months at Trinity a picture of me with a young man from Georgetown appeared on the front page of the Washington Post. We were intently talking to each other at a football game, and the caption read, "What game?" This was not a good impression for a freshman girl to give to her new professors.

Most of the girls had been to prep school, so they had an advantage with study skills and time management. About a third of the girls at Trinity were from foreign countries, and their fathers were mainly employed by foreign embassies. The cosmopolitan environment fascinated me. I became friends with a girl from Pakistan named Iran. One night, she invited me to dinner at the Embassy of Pakistan. The embassy was beautiful. The dining room was large and gracious, the table was set with elegant things, and the carpets were magnificent. Everyone there made me feel welcome.

At the table were Iran's parents, another couple, and a young boy. They all engaged in a lively conservation that I did not understand. The young boy said something to his father that made everyone laugh and look at me with smiles. Iran apologized to me, but then she explained that her brother had pointed at me and said to his father, "I will take her to keep." There was a silence, and then I looked at the young boy and said, "Not yet," which created more laughter.

That year at Trinity, I met girls from Poland, Puerto Rico, Ireland, Chile, Syria, China, India, Pakistan, Columbia, Germany, The Philippines, Lithuania, and France. I was not inspired to really concentrate on academics. I do not remember any really outstanding lecturer, and I received mediocre grades. Many things I learned at Trinity, however, stayed with me. I had decided not to continue college there. Eleven years of Catholic schools was enough. I wanted to go to a large public university.

My parents were disappointed that I didn't want to stay another year. I also didn't want to go to Purdue, where my father was teaching. Neither living at home again nor being a professor's daughter on the campus were appealing to me. I had visited Indiana University in Bloomington while my brother was a student there, and I had found the campus very beautiful with simple limestone buildings and a great variety of trees. I.U. offered a wide range of career choices and interesting activities, and it gave an impression of freedom. If I was not academically challenged at I.U., it would be my own fault. I had decided that was where I wanted to go. My father did not like the idea at all. He thought the University was too large, that I was to inexperienced to deal with it, and that I would get lost in the shuffle.

Nevertheless, I enrolled that year at I.U. as a sophomore, and the next three years were the happiest of my young life. During my first semester, I lived in a dormitory for girls. The second semester, the Sorority Rush (a series of parties) began, and I entered it with reservations. I knew next to nothing about sororities, except that many of those who applied were not accepted. To my great joy and surprise, I was asked to join the sorority of my first choice, Kappa Alpha Theta. I was thrilled to be asked to join even though I was not a legacy, no one had recommended me, and there was nothing exceptional about me.

At Kappa Alpha Theta, I found a home and lifelong friends. This sorority has been among the best with regard to academic rating, and its culture created strong incentives for studying and achieving good grades. I was comfortable at I.U.

I majored in Elementary Education to prepare for a teaching career. I took interesting courses with some excellent teachers, received good grades, and was awarded a Bachelor of Arts degree. I also had an active social life and met my future husband. After graduation, I taught sixth grade in Indianapolis for a year. That summer, I experienced one of my life's highlights that was never to be forgotten - I went to Europe with my best friend.

"I can go," said Carrie with excitement.

"Really? For sure?" I shouted back.

I had called Carrie, my best girlfriend and former college roommate, to see if she wanted to spend the summer in Europe with me, taking a class at the Sorbonne in Paris and driving around Europe. We were both teaching school in different cities. Our serious relationships were in the wings, and at that time, a wedding wasn't a consideration for either of us.

"We need to share the planning."

"What date shall we shoot for?"

"We need a program of classes from the Sorbonne and a place to live."

"Dad said we'll need an international driver's license."

"I've heard driving in Paris and Rome is really scary."

"Let's find out for ourselves," one of us said bravely.

The plans were made and we were sailing on Cunard's ship, Scythia. We had been accepted to take a class at the Sorbonne and would live at the CITE, a house for international students that were attending the Sorbonne.

We were twenty years old and not very sophisticated in the ways of the world, but we were ready to learn. Our light blue eyes, brown hair, slender young bodies, and ready smiles gave us away immediately as young, eager, and enthusiastic American women with a mission - to have a good time. Sailing the Atlantic was great fun. We soaked up the sun from our deck chairs as we read. At night, we giggled over our before-dinner martinis. We made a pact to always stick together on this trip.

There was a visit with Isabelle in London, where she showed us the sights. We promised ourselves that we'd have to come back to London another time. We were getting used to our small Renault. It was easy to drive, and its small size had some definite advantages.

The day before we left Isabelle, she said she had a favor to ask of us. "A cousin of mine is here from Buenos Aires on business and needs a ride to the French Riviera."

Carrie and I both shrugged our shoulders. "What is her name?"

"Peter Eisner," Isabelle answered.

"A guy?" we both said in unison.

The next day Carrie, Peter, and I piled into the little Renault. Peter offered to drive, but we declined. Along the way we all shared the small bedrooms. Carrie and I always slept in the same bed. The three of us went to mass together, and we visited a famous synagogue along the way. The casino in Monte Carlo was exciting, and we all enjoyed walking around as if we belonged there. Saint Tropez on the Riviera was the destination, and what a destination it was! This was before Brigitte Bardot made her appearance, and the place was relatively calm. Upon our first appearance at the beach, Peter looked horrified. "Come on girls, we're going across the street. I'm buying you two bathing suits." I personally felt insulted. I had bought my beautiful, ballet-style suit at Saks Fifth Avenue, and I thought Carrie's beautiful blue suit with the little skirt was perfect, too - little skirts were so flattering. After ten minutes on the beach and a multitude of stares, however, we realized that our wonderful suits were just too much. We followed Peter across the street to a shop. Neither of us had ever worn a bikini before. Carrie chose a little suit in pink and white check. I chose the same suit in blue and white check. Peter smiled his approval as we went back to the beach. My ballet suit was later stolen at the "CITE," where I left it to dry one day. Our bikinis became a favorite possession for that season.

Peter was giving us mixed signals in regards to any romantic interests. He didn't play favorites. The night before he left, he asked me to go for a walk with him. This resulted in a lovely kiss. As he pulled me close to him, he said, "Come away with me."

"Where?" I asked in a whisper.

"To Buenos Aires."

"I can't do that! My parents would be furious, and I signed a teaching contract for the fall." He leaned back and looked at me with a smile.

"Don't ever change. I will remember you always."

Peter is a happy memory that I still have to this day.

Happiness - could there be more in the lives of two young girls in the 1950s?

L'Abbe in Paris, was our favorite cafe. There were two male vocalists that charmed us with their ballads.

Driving in Rome was a challenge but we did well. We met handsome men who wanted to show us around. We saw a great deal and always stuck together.

Chartes in France was our favorite church, but the Basilica in Rome was awesome. We went back the following summer with new itineraries and adventures to experience. What happy, carefree girls we were!

City Hospital

That February day was cold and bleak. Grandmother from Shelbyville came to stay with the children. She and I became very good friends over many years. The old Ford station wagon purred along and spewed out as much heat as it could handle on our trip to Indianapolis.

Saying that Will and I were brave that day would be a lie. I had agreed that my life was out of control and that I would be a patient at a short-term psychiatric hospital. Looking back, it doesn't seem possible that I thought this was necessary.

I was a thirty-one-year-old woman who loved my family deeply. My marriage was only six years old. Try to imagine what it was like that early morning for me to say goodbye bravely to my six week-old baby who needed my milk and goodbye to my other two sons as well, who begged to go. My heart broke and shattered at this departure. We needed each other. Could we survive this? I wondered to myself.

I can't pretend to tell you about our arrival at the hospital or much about the whole experience. I have no visual memories of the building or being greeted and admitted, nor do I have memories of saying goodbye to my precious Will. It is all a blank. I wish I could jauntily say, "Forgetting those six months isn't all bad." I cannot say that, however, because it is like losing an important piece to a puzzle and always searching for it.

As a resident there, I lost a youthful lightness forever. It seems as if in that year of nineteen hundred and sixty-two, I became an experiment for very young doctors and nurses. They were going to cure me. Cure me of what? A sailing accident, neurosurgery that left me paralyzed, the Cuban Crisis, having my newborn baby taken away, or postpartum depression? No one talked to me, no one listened, and no one even tried to understand. How could they know what to do? Would a book tell them?

There was some peace for me because I knew Willy and John were with my parents in Michigan, and Tom was with his grandparents in Shelbyville. I knew my sons were being well taken care of.

I don't know where I slept or ate, and I don't know the color of the walls or furniture. There is not a single face that I can remember in those six months. I do remember a room full of cots on wheels. Three days a week in the early morning, we came to this room in a loose robe. I don't know how we found our appointed cot because we were so frightened. It was a gut-wrenching, limb-shaking, nauseating fear. If "it" was there, we couldn't leave the room. "It" was a foul-smelling, very short gown that had to be put on. We stood before each other and changed from the robe to the gown, then sat waiting in the very cool room. A person would walk by, ask us to lie down, and give us a shot. We waited, trembling. We learned to behave like senseless, vapid women. After awhile, a person would push a cot into a small room.. There would be people waiting there. They were so young that I wondered at times whether they were students from the nearby medical school. I don't remember anyone saying anything, but I distinctly remember someone pushing a hard rubber thing into my mouth. One time, a person said, "Wait," and the piece was readjusted in my mouth. Later, I learned that this prevented the patient from biting off her tongue or lip as the surge of electricity went through the body and convulsed the muscles violently. I never felt pain during this process, but I was terrified each time. This therapy is called Electric Shock Therapy, or E.S.T. The mental confusion and fuzziness after this treatment was all-consuming for most of the remaining day. Memories from the past were never to be regained. One could see the effects of these "treatments" on patients as they walked in a state of confusion and forgetfulness. They did not know where they were, where they had been, or where they were going.

No one came to see me during this time, as it would have been fruitless. I don't remember a conversation with anyone - doctor, nurse or other patient. There were times on "off" days when we went to occupational therapy to make craft items. For many years, I kept a ceramic hotplate that I made during therapy. I tried to embroider a pair of pillowcases with blue thread. These projects were a good distraction from the confusion and also encouraged one to think about returning home with these treasures.

Eventually, Will began to visit me. We could go to a room where there were small tables and an ice cream bar for ice cream. By that time, he had moved to Indianapolis and joined a prestigious law firm. He found a modest house near a good elementary school. Willy could walk to school with the neighborhood children. My eyes burned and my chest ached because I had not been a part of these monumentally important times.

Will was so brave and so tired. The transition from being a student to working in a firm must have been overwhelming with three children and no wife to help. Will must have been doubtful about my progress and future as a helpmate in our young family.

My dearest children, I'll never know what it was like for you during this time. I do know that you were well-cared for by your father, grandparents, and three uncles.

One morning, a great commotion swept through the hospital - a woman was found dead in the street, wearing only her small hospital gown. In a state of confusion she had slipped out of a side door and walked down the side steps into the dazzling sunlight. It was rush hour, and the street traffic was heavy. Hopefully, she never knew what hit her. I overheard a hospital aide tell another, "Her eyes and mouth looked like an animal hit and dead on the side of the road." My stomach revolted. Apparently the press didn't learn the true facts, or if they did, they never printed them. This kind of incident is not soon forgotten.

I never knew what determined that I was ready to go home. One day, seemingly out of the blue, a smiling Will said he had come to take me home to our first home in Indianapolis. At first, I felt great ambition and expectations. Then, as the time approached, I began to worry. My palms became sweaty and my throat was dry. Maybe he didn't need or want me any more. He had found his own way for six months now. We greeted each other warmly just like old times, but things were very different for both of us. I was surprised to see the new car - a big, very shiny, navy blue Oldsmobile. It was being leased for Will by his law firm. I was taken aback that our station wagon had been disposed of without my knowing. "Of course," I scolded myself. "One wouldn't expect an attorney with a good firm to drive a beat-up old station wagon. How stupid not to think of that!"

"So this is where we live now? It's just right for all of us," I said as we entered the small limestone house with a fenced-in backyard on Indianola Street. "Welcome home! It's small, a rental, and temporary, but it's ours," he said, and I loved him for saying "ours."

"Let's get you inside. My mom has Willy and Tom in Shelbyville, and they'll be here late tomorrow morning. John will be back from Michigan soon," he explained.

Going into the house frightened me. Things were different now, and I was anxious. What would we do in there? Our lives and bed had not been shared for a long time. There was a feeling of strangeness between us. Carefully, I picked my way through the gravel driveway, through the grass, and up the two front steps. I hadn't had any major incidents in falling or knocking anything over for a while now. Were the neighbors watching? They must have wondered where their new neighbor's wife was. Had he told them that I had been in a mental hospital for the past six months having electric shock treatment? Had he told them that I was awkward and fell over my own feet, or that I could have a major seizure at any time because of brain damage? Oh my God, I don't belong in a normal neighborhood with normal people. I could feel myself becoming anxious and was relieved when Will said, "I've got a conference at the office in an hour. Will you be okay?"

"Oh, sure. I'll take a shower, shampoo my hair, and unpack. I'll check out the fridge and see if I can stir up something for dinner." This all made sense. It's what I did after returning home from the hospital with a baby. I saw signs of relief sweep over Will's face. Well, what did he expect? I thought to myself.

My heart sank when he called back, "Oh, Sharon from next door might stop over. She's anxious to welcome you to the neighborhood." \

"How nice," I responded brightly, closing the door.

The room became eerily quiet. I hadn't been in a room by myself for a long time. I lit a cigarette and sat down. When I had entered the hospital, I smoked very little - maybe two cigarettes a day. After leaving the hospital, I was up to nearly a pack a day. The familiar blue blanket felt good as I sat comfortably on the worn sofa that we had bought in Dover, Delaware, before Willy's birth. The two nicely-framed photographs across the room made me smile. One was from a fraternity party in Bloomington, the year Will and I met. The other was of Will looking very handsome in his flight suit, standing in front of the C-130 which he flew.

Will and Sonia

During my second semester at I.U., I met a young man with whom I would have a long and complicated relationship. I had a phone call from a boy who had been a high school classmate.

Sonia

"Hey, Sonia. I've got a fraternity brother who would like to meet you. He saw you in the library the other day."

"Hmm, what's he like?" I asked cautiously.

"He's a nice guy and really good-looking."

"Sure. Who you think is good-looking might be different from what I'd think."

"Trust me. How about meeting at the commons at three o'clock Wednesday?"

"Will you both be there?"

"If that's what you want. Bye."

We were both pleased at what we saw. Will was tall and slim. He had dark brown eyes that had a wonderful twinkle. His hair was dark and shiny, but best of all, he had two wonderful and deep dimples. I liked his shy smile. He had an accent that was unfamiliar to me. I later learned that the accent was characteristic of the area of southern Indiana from which he had come. He had joined a well-respected fraternity and was ready to begin a new life. He waited on tables at his frat house to help pay the fees for living there, so he had less free time than most of his brothers.

We began to date steadily that semester. I had other dates now and then, but they didn't last long. One of the most endearing things about Will was his sense of humor. It was understated, and the retorts were quick and clever. People laughed especially at his self-deprecating one-liners that became his signature, making fun of his "dirt poor farm boy background with all its disadvantages."

The Moving Finger

We saw each other regularly on weekends. I had "study table" six nights a week, since my sorority's rules required that those with unproven grades study from at least seven to ten on weeknights. My house was serious about scholarship, which was good for me after my experience at Trinity.

My cultural activities, however, became almost non-existent, and I began missing them. Will had little interest in ballet, symphonies, operas, and speakers, but I increasingly found others to go with me. Oh, well! We had other things in common. He also had no interest in reading for leisure, as I had always done and enjoyed, but what difference did that make?

Will invited me to his home to meet his parents and brothers. They were very warm and cordial to me. I was impressed by their beautifully manicured lawn and spacious home. Their town was small, and they appeared to be one of its most prosperous families. The coordinated fabrics on furniture and windows were lovely and fresh, but I was not yet accustomed to light-colored wall-to-wall carpeting. The family had moved to this town from a much smaller one so that Will could attend a larger high school. I have some very happy memories of Will's family and their home.

I had been raised in the Catholic church, while Will had been raised as a Methodist and Baptist. His father had been a Quaker. All of these were a basis for a strict upbringing.

Before we graduated, I met a fellow named Lou. We had a lot in common, and I even accepted his fraternity pin. That was the closest I came from drifting away from Will. That fall, I went to Indianapolis for my first teaching assignment. Lou was there in medical school, and Will was completing his senior year in Bloomington. He came to see me in Indianapolis when he had the chance. That summer, and again the following summer, I went to Europe with Carrie.

After I returned from Europe and resumed teaching in Indianapolis, I shared an apartment with my friend, Anne. She had lived across the lake from me in the summer and was also teaching. Will had been active in ROTC in college and would be going into the Air Force for three years after graduation.

It was a cool Sunday, and I was grading my students' papers and calculating grade averages for the report cards due the next week. I loved my job. The students were great kids. They were doing well. My school was in a neat, middle-class neighborhood on the city's south side, and I traveled to work easily, taking a bus in front of my apartment building and transferring downtown. The phone rang. It was Will. His father had some serious legal problems, and Will was trying to take care of them. He was very upset and needed help. We began to date again and became a couple. Upon his graduation from I.U., he entered the Air Force as he had planned. He was posted in Dover, Delaware. We were married in Lafayette, and then we left for Dover.

Our small and simple wedding was in St. Mary's Cathedral. My mother had made my lovely gown (think Audrey Hepburn) and the gowns of my four attendants. Our reception was held in our spacious backyard. We left the reception for Dover, Delaware, which was our home for the next three years. Upon arriving in Chicago, we learned that the next five hours would be spent waiting for our connection to Dover.

We had a wonderful time in Dover and in the Air Force. We had advantages since Will was an Officer. We used the commissary for most of our shopping and the Officer's Club for entertainment. The "Wife's Club" was a good meeting place when husbands were off on a trip.

I had decided to teach school in the Dover School system. We had pledged to save as much money as we could for graduate school. Will's mother was alone now with her youngest son, and she had very little support. We sent a monthly check to her, and we felt fortunate that we could do so.

Our first little rented house was very modest and furnished with the bare necessities. Our car was old, but that didn't bother us. We thought of the future, our whole lives ahead of us, and the perks that we would earn together. We planted a small garden of vegetables and flowers. There was a large clothesline in the yard where our laundry dried. Next door, there was a wonderful big yellow tomcat named Manlove. It was true love between us. The Amish had a farmer's market across the dusty street from us, which was always a source of interest. We heated our little red, tarpaper house by turning on some gas, throwing a lit match down a hole in the floor, and then holding our breath. These were magical years. We were young, with college behind us, and in love.

Sonia

For years, the memories of our first Thanksgiving and Christmas together brought back floods of sentiment and tenderness. Our small round table, two chairs, and bed were unfinished furniture from Sears, and they served us well. Our lives were simple, and our home was uncluttered with things. In the evenings, we walked down the dusty road hand-in-hand with Manlove trotting behind with his yellow bushy tail up like a flag. We went to Rehoboth Beach and played in the ocean before cooking a seafood meal on the beach with friends. At Christmas, we bought trees that filled our small room with the fragrance that we both loved, and we exchanged our small gifts.

Will looked so handsome in his crisp uniforms. I was in awe of the C-130. It was enormous in size. It carried troops, jeeps, and other equipment to all parts of the world. One day, I watched Will climb into the pilot's seat and take off from the runway. "I had better stop being so bossy," I thought to myself.

When I was told that I was pregnant for sure with our first child, I told Will, and we danced around the room in pure joy. We moved to Base Housing after that. There was more money coming in, and it was cleaner and more convenient. Willy was born in 1959, followed by Tom in 1961 during early Law School days.

When Will's three years of active duty were over, we moved back to Bloomington, Indiana, where he began his law studies. My boating accident and operation soon followed.

4. Central State Hospital

Eleanor Roosevelt once said, "You gain strength, courage, and confidence by every experience in which you really stop to look fear in the face. You must do the thing you think you cannot do."

In my experience, "looking fear in the face" and moving on have been the keys to my good health and survival under very stressful experiences.

I Agree to Enter Central State

I had been seeing Dr. Clare, a psychiatrist off and on since we had moved to Indianapolis after Will's graduation from law school. He was very warm and friendly to both of us in an almost fatherly manner. He had a large, square head on his medium-tall, stocky frame, as well as a ready smile and a quick sense of humor. I found him very appealing. The gray hair and lined face reflected years of experience.

As much as I liked him, however, I wasn't prepared for what he suggested on one of our last visits. "I know you are discouraged, and I have a suggestion," he said gently. "You have spent six months in a short-term hospital with a series of shock treatments. During the past several years, you have been a patient in the psychiatric ward of Methodist Hospital. There you had two more series of shock treatments for depression. The private hospital in Louisville, Kentucky, stabilized you for a short time, even after you refused to take the insulin-induced coma treatments that they recommended. We have tried all of the antidepressants that we think are suitable for you. Will you agree to Central State Hospital?"

With a choking feeling in my throat and a sick feeling in my stomach, I nodded as my eyes were blinded with burning tears. "I have never refused your recommendations, nor have I ever been forced to do anything I disagreed with," I said numbly, "but this seems like a sentence."

"It won't be. This illness will be eased in time," he said with conviction.

"How could I have failed so miserably?" I asked myself repeatedly.

I had spent the past several years with my family, doing all the things that are expected of a wife and mother, including: cooking meals, keeping house, looking after my children, meeting with their teachers, sleeping with my husband, occasionally entertaining and going out, and going to Walloon in the summer. Yet, I was miserable. I felt constantly pressured, overwhelmed, boxed in, inadequate, and obviously depressed. There was no sign of improvement, and my relationship with my husband worsened.

The First Four Weeks

Will and I sadly agreed that I should be admitted to Central State Hospital in the interest of both my long-term health and the stability of the family. We drove in silence to the hospital, knowing that we would be separated for a long time. I was tormented with thoughts about what I might have done, yet I knew that I had really tried hard to be normal.

As we drove through the tall metal gates into the large hospital grounds, it didn't appear that much was going on. Everything looked old and shabby. The buildings, even the trees, were in a state of decay, except for the admitting building, which was new. We rang the bell and the door was unlocked. My heart sank further when an officious-looking woman looked at my paperwork. Without a word, she ushered us in.

"What's all that?" she asked with a glance at my rather handsome bags, which contained clothes, a hair dryer, a radio, makeup, nail polish, and other "necessities." In as pert a voice as I could muster, I said, "Those are the things I'll need." With a tight smile on her face, she said in a sarcastic voice, "You won't need none of that stuff, girl. We furnish even your clothes. No stuck-up stuff goes on here. No, it sure don't." Looking at Will, she said "You can take all that stuff home now."

As two large black women entered the room, she told me to go with them. We walked down a long, cold hall. The gray cement was unrelenting in its starkness. The electricity in the parting look Will and I had given each other was still vibrating in my mind. We entered a dank-smelling room. The largest woman told me to remove my clothes, as I was to take a shower.

"Oh, I took a shower this morning."

"Not like the one you're going to have now," she said evenly. My heart began to beat uncontrollably, and thoughts of the gas chamber passed through my mind.

"You can put your clothes there," one of the women said with a grin. As I took off my clothes, I folded them neatly on the metal chair. "We need some neatness around here. You won't need that stuff, though - not for a long time."

I was ushered into a large metal shower stall. Hot water washed over my body before a dark, green liquid was poured over my head. I immediately recognized the smell. It was an ordinary disinfectant, like they used in the public schools where I worked. A woman with a large rubber apron began to scrub my head. Did they think I had lice? Perhaps they did. The rest of me was scrubbed with the help of another pair of hands. How humiliating the process was. I was finally handed a small gray towel. Clothing had been placed on the rusty metal chair. At that point, any clothes looked good. The panties and bra hung loosely on me. The worn cotton skirt and blouse should have been cleaning rags. The gray socks fit pretty well, but the shoes were much too small. I had no comb, so running my cold fingers through my hair was the best that I could do. I was beginning a new chapter in my life.

After the shower, I was ushered into a medium-sized common room. There was some worn furniture where twelve women were sitting or standing. They were all smoking. The back section of the room was used by attendants and aides to do paperwork and discuss their wards. Upon entering, I was dizzy from the smell of tobacco smoke. I had smoked lightly in college, but this room in which I spent most daytime hours for six weeks, must have been the unhealthiest environment of my life.

I can still visualize the young woman who called out, "Here she comes!" as I entered the room. Her name was Mary, and we remained friends until the day she disappeared. This room was used as living quarters by women entering the hospital, where they could be under constant observation for six weeks. These rooms constituted a locked ward from which no one could leave unescorted. Our meals were brought to the room. My dominant memory is one of unending boredom, with nothing to do except smoke. My wardmates moaned, wept, and rocked. There were no visitors or mail. All medications that had been used by the inmates were suspended, resulting in a wide range of problems. I could never do justice in describing the food, but suffice it to say that I weighed one hundred twenty-five pounds when I entered the hospital and ninety-five pounds when I left it. There were fights, often over food or misunderstandings. There were also threats, screams for help, constant smoking, and card games that I had never played before. People were dragged in and dragged out. Inmates suffered from a wide variety of problems and illnesses. Those who coped stopped thinking, prayed a lot, and concentrated on survival.

Conference Day

The first four weeks dragged in the observation ward. The boredom never ceased. The magazines had been almost memorized. There were two attendants that occasionally brought in different magazines, which eased their boredom, too. Card playing was a distraction, and I learned several games that were fun as long as there were no arguments. It became obvious that some people were having behavioral and physical problems without their former medications or habits.

During this time, I had a seizure while I was sitting on the floor near my new friend, Mary. I was terrified of this happening, and it had worried me since I was no longer taking Dilantin. Dr. Clare told me a long time ago that I might need Dilantin for the rest of my life because of the scar tissue on my brain due to surgery.

I woke up with my head in Mary's lap, and people were staring at me. An attendant was giving orders, and there was an unusual quietness in the room. I started to sit up and then realized what had happened. "Oh, no," I said as my heart was racing uncontrollably. This was my greatest fear - the fear that consumed me almost constantly. "It's all right. It's all right," crooned Mary. "This used to happen to my boss. I know about this." This eased me somewhat. A special relationship grew between us because of this incident.

I had never seen anyone have a seizure, but I was sure it was hideous. Being out of control in any way was bad enough, but to jerk around (and whatever else happened) was absolutely unforgivable. Within a short time, my medication was reinstated. There has been only one more seizure since that happened, but at

The Moving Finger

the time even the slightest possibility was terrifying. Who would take care of my small children? What about driving, swimming, skiing, making love, teaching school, taking trips, volunteering, going to parties, and having parties? How could one live at all with this overhanging threat?

Another happening that is as vivid now as it was over forty years ago that I still feel shame about is the fact that I became a predator. I saw the woman open the worn brown paper bag, and then she took out a small package of cake. It was the dry kind with rubbery chocolate frosting and the white sugary filling in the middle. Never had I coveted anything so much in my life. The cheap cake tormented me. I had seen the man who had brought her the package through the door. He looked very kind and solemn. I watched where she put the bag on the floor near her old flowered pillow. Later that day, I positioned myself near the pillow.

It wasn't until the following day that I put my hand in the bag with great care and a racing heart. The box of cakes was open, and I took out a small package carefully. I quietly opened my prize. It was stale and rubbery, but it gave me something no words can explain. After rolling up the paper carefully and putting it in my pocket, I looked up. An aide was watching me, and I almost threw up. She had a small superior smile on her large lips. Her eyes would not leave mine, the smile would not fade. She had watched me steal. I was now a common thief. The incident was never mentioned, but that didn't take away the kind of shame I felt. I felt like a young child being caught doing something naughty.

There was an electric feeling in the air on my conference day. Apparently, this was the day that a decision would be made about what to do with me next. A group of outside consultants came on days specifically set aside for this purpose to interview patients. I had seen other patients get ready for this interview, treating it as a very special occasion. An attendant fooled with my hair, arranging it this way and that. I was encouraged to use a little lipstick, and then I was given the clothes I had worn on the day I had arrived. Apparently how I looked would make a difference to this group.

I remember entering a room with a man and three women. The man stood and asked me to sit down on a chair facing them. He introduced me to the women, and then he introduced himself. There was a terrible moment after he asked me why I was there; I couldn't think of the words to answer his question. "Was it anxiety and depression?" he asked. I said "Yes," probably too loudly, but I was so relieved to have an answer. I don't remember the rest of the conference, but I do know that I was not very involved. They talked in an earnest, officious kind of way, and they seemed to know each other well as they laughed in a familiar way.

The next day, an attendant said, "Congratulations! You are being sent to the Women's Building after breakfast!"

I asked, "Does Dr. Clare know about this? What about my husband?"

She looked at me as if she hadn't heard me correctly. "You just don't get it, do you? It really don't matter what they think. Now get your stuff together, girl." I numbly realized that it was true. I probably did appear ridiculous to think someone else had a say in

The Moving Finger

what was already planned for me. I said goodbye to Mary, as she was my only friend. We were both tearful. We made no gestures of affection. A hug could be misunderstood by others. Any display of emotion was dangerous here.

After breakfast, two attendants that I did not recognize escorted me to the infamous Women's Building. It was a large, five-story building that was one hundred years old, and it looked and smelled like it, too. The windows had metal bars on them, and the stairs looked like marble with metal reinforcements. The steps were worn by the feet of the sane and insane women that had lived there over the many years. They would drag their broken minds and bodies up these steps year after year. After all, it was a long-term mental hospital.

As we entered, I was overwhelmed by the smell of the damp decay. We walked up several flights of narrow, steep steps. On two occasions, I saw women being taken out of the building. One was screaming at the top of her lungs. The other one looked like a dead woman walking. I will never forget her face.

Every floor had a ward. Some were called "locked" wards. The one I was going to was open. The patients there walked in and out as they pleased. Everyone on that ward had an eight-hour job, five or six days a week, without pay. I didn't know where I would be working. I had been warned about the laundry and kitchen. Mary said that those were the back- and spirit-breaking jobs and that I should pray for something better.

We reached the floor I would call home for over a year. The smells were staggering, but there wasn't the smell of people smoking. There were rocking chairs and sofas that were old and tattered. The round tables were there for card playing during off hours. There were thirty women living on this floor. I was introduced to the attendant in charge. She seemed very pleasant. After the three aides had discussed me and the head attendant had looked over my paperwork, she showed me where I would sleep.

The Women's Building

We walked into a dormitory-type room with nine metal cots. On top of the thin mattress were gray sheets, a pitiful pillow, and a thin and rough blanket with holes. How could it be that bad? It was that bad. Thousands of women like me have experienced such conditions throughout the country due to no fault of their own. There was also a small towel and wash cloth, which were, of course, also gray. Next to each bed was a small metal table for one's meager belongings. After leaving the observation ward, we were allowed to wear our own clothes, although many women continued to wear the clothing that was issued to them upon arrival. We hung our extra things on a taut rope in a large room. It was difficult to determine what belonged to whom, although this generally worked out.

The attendant asked me to sit at a round table for a briefing. She said, "Life here will be pretty much what you want to make of it. Cooperate and keep your nose clean, and living here will be bearable. Cause trouble, and your life will be hell on earth. Here are the rules: Breakfast is at seven o'clock sharp, lunch is at twelve-thirty, and supper is at six. If you miss mealtime, you go without. Sonia, your bath time is seven o'clock sharp, and you are to be out seven minutes later when the next person in line walks in. We have thirty women and one tub, and that's the way it is. The cleanser and soap will be there. If you are off work and no baths are scheduled, there is a bucket for washing your hair and clothes. It gets tight, but it all seems to get done. There's a drying room behind the clothes room. No hairdresser or laundry service around here; never was. Don't lose your bath towel, or you go without for the rest of the week. Oh yes, don't keep any money or anything else you can't live without laying around, because it will probably get stolen and there are no detectives. I do have some good news for you," she continued. "You'll be working at the canteen. A nice woman from the outside runs it. There are always two patients working with her. This is the best patient job in the whole place. You don't get paid, but it's a good place to spend your days. Don't ever spout off to anybody or steal anything, or you'll get the axe."

I thought about the dry chocolate cake with guilt, but during the time I worked at the canteen, I never missed a day or was late. It was my salvation.

I can remember clearly leaving for the canteen that first day. I had groomed myself the best that I could with very few things. As I walked down the many steps past the other wards, the usual sounds could be heard - yelling, crying, doors slamming, key rattling, and rocking chairs going back and forth. A few people were sitting on the narrow steps in varying degrees of disorder. One woman pulled on the hem of my skirt, pointed to something, and chuckled - a rat the size of a cat was watching us. Bile rose in my throat. A lot of large rats lived with us in this very old, large building. I hurried on down to the fresh air.

I reveled in my good fortune. I could come and go as I pleased, and I had a good job that I would do well. The canteen was a clean, bright building, and the person in charge was intelligent and healthy. Mrs. R. was a large, handsome, professional-looking woman. She had the reputation for taking no nonsense from anyone who came into her shop. She never raised her voice if someone was out of control and creating a disturbance. She could stop a fight with a few well-chosen words, and if that didn't work, she would signal to another employee to usher out the offending party. As a consequence, he or she was not to return to the canteen. I wondered where this woman had come from, what her story was, and what circumstances had made her so suitable for running a canteen for the mentally ill. I never found out.

One day, Mrs. R. told me that a new worker was coming to the canteen soon. A few days later, my friend Mary walked in. We both had broad smiles on her arrival, and we touched hands. I hadn't seen her in weeks.

An Incident

I didn't sleep well that night. Mary hadn't returned yet from her leave. We were planning to work with Mrs. R. after work while she did an inventory of her merchandise. It was another busy day, and there had been no major incidents. It was all of the indecisions and deliberations that had made the day seem long. The sad and confused faces along with the loud and strident voices of the attendants became irritating at times, but usually a deep breath and a distraction of some kind eased the tension. That day, two older retarded men became a source of amusement for two attendants. They intentionally created more confusion than was necessary. One of the men finally sat on the floor with his head in his hands and sobbed in frustration. I bit my tongue to keep from making a protest. Later, I learned that Mrs. R. reported such incidents to whomever would listen.

Mrs. R. (we never called her by any other name) told me that since we were working late, she had brought a picnic supper. My spirits soared. "Is Mary going to be late?" I asked her.

"No. She didn't come back last night." She gave me a concerned glance.

"I know," I said.

The supper was wonderful. Baby Swiss cheese and ham were between an unusually good rye bread. The potato salad was cold and fresh. We had butterscotch brownies and hot coffee for dessert. I wondered if she knew what a precious treat this was for me.

It had almost gotten dark outside except for a few street lights here and there. "Would you like for me to call someone to walk back with you?"

"Are you kidding? Nothing scares me around here anymore," I said with bravado.

I had almost reached the entrance when someone grabbed me from behind. "Scream and I'll kill you!" said a husky male voice. Within several seconds, I had been dragged into the bushes and was flat on my back. A metal pipe dug cruelly into my back. The large man on top of me was tearing at my clothes. "Please don't!" I begged. His fist hit me in the mouth, and the taste of blood shocked me.

"What the hell, man?" said a familiar voice. It was Andy, one of the aides. With that, my attacker mumbled, "Shit!" He was gone into the bushes.

Andy looked me over and asked, "You all right?"

"No, I'm not alright. I was almost raped."

"Don't tell anybody about this yet, y'hear?"

"You have to be kidding!" I said angrily.

"You do, and you'll be fair game here for some guys. That fool was just walking through to see what he could find."

"He found me," I mumbled tearfully.

I reluctantly left for work the next day. My back ached where the pipe had dug into it last night, and the inside of my mouth felt raw from the blow. I hadn't told anyone about the incident the night before. Who was there to tell? A female attendant was approaching me and signaled for me to follow her. "Andy called me last night and told me about what happened to you. The guy wasn't from here, Andy never saw him before. "But that doesn't help me much, does it?" I mumbled.

She said, "So whatta ya going to do?" "Well, you could call the police or the newspaper. You'd become an instant celebrity. How about that? Front page stuff, "Local woman raped on grounds of local hospital."

"Oh, no. I've embarrassed my family enough. Not that."

"Well, honey, I can tell you one thing worse. If you went public, there's some guy here that would find you and finish the job."

This really made me mad. "I'm telling my husband, and he'll know what to do."

"I'll save copies of the newspaper for you. How many do you want? You can send them to your friends. I've been here for fourteen years and I'm telling you to forget it!"

I looked into her sympathetic brown eyes, as mine welled with tears, and said, "I've forgotten it."

The Canteen

After working at the canteen for a few months, I became aware of something that touched me deeply. Gifts were being bought by patients for patients. Some of those forgotten people were looking for new relationships. They felt rejected by family and society, and the most likely way to reach out was with a small gift - here, notice me, I like you, like children in grade school.

There were a number of gifts that cost less than a dollar - a comb, a candy bar, a pen, or a small piece of costume jewelry. With patients allowed to have no more than $3 per week in spending money, such gifts made a strong statement.

We saw relationships develop into hand-holding (there was also a Men's Building on the grounds, and the men also used the canteen), and news circulated fast about who was going with whom. Sometimes visiting family members responded with ridicule or anger when they were innocently introduced to the new "boyfriend" or "girlfriend," not realizing what basic need was being filled by the innocent overtures. One couple had "gone together" for over ten years. Some people that were there for life had the good fortune to find someone who cared about them and who they could love in their special way.

Addie

She was only a slip of a woman and not young, with thin and knotted legs that showed muscle and veins from her energetic moves. She had been at the hospital for twelve years and had no place else to go. Everyone knew Addie, as she was always pleasant and willing to please. I never knew if she had a job at the hospital. She was in and out of the canteen, often spending a nickel or dime.

Addie served in her own way. There was a fast food restaurant several blocks away. For a nickel or a dime, Addie would run to the restaurant to fill orders for the aides, or sometimes for a fortunate patient. She would return winded, with a smile of achievement on her small pinched-up face.

Addie was called "slow-witted." It was an achievement for her to keep the orders and the money straight. How she managed the busy streets and not being taken advantage of still remains a mystery. It was her panting for breath and the smile of accomplishment that has stayed in my memory.

One night the smile faded. She returned with several greasy bags of food sending out its unique aroma and gave them to an aide. They exchanged words, and Addie walked away slowly. Her long, gray hair hung in her face, and her shoulders slumped. Suddenly, she sat on a step and cried racking sobs. She hadn't received the dime she had been promised, and she was too late for her own miserable meal in the dining hall. It was yet another injustice to someone who **had tried so hard to please.**

A Short-Term Roommate

Would she sit up again and watch? What was it that she watched with those haunted, vacant eyes? I began to worry. The night before, I had heard the ancient metal bed springs protest the shifting of her weight. I watched her through mostly closed eyes with the dim light under the plywood door. She leaned on her elbow as she studied the rest of us in the small, cramped room. She was the newest arrival, and I never heard her utter or even murmur a word of any kind. Maybe she couldn't speak. I knew she could hear because I had heard the night attendant berate her about her refusal to take her night medication.

During that night, she was especially restless as she twirled her matted, stringy brown hair in her fingers. She knelt on the floor by her bed, lowered her head, and folded her hands as if she was praying. Although I was exhausted, I slipped in and out of sleep. Every time that I woke up, I saw that she was on the cold floor in her skimpy gown with her head a little lower. When I left for work in the morning, she was on the floor with her pitiful gray blanket over her.

When I returned from work, our new roommate was gone. She never appeared again. We could only speculate about what had happened to her.

The Dance

Working at the canteen was wonderful therapy for me. My day was structured and I was able to do something I liked, and it was always under good conditions. Eventually, other patients and attendants began calling me by name. Two male attendants were becoming more familiar than I was comfortable with, so I more or less ignored them. Since they were sometimes "in charge" of us, however, I remained polite, cool, and quiet with them. Some of the female attendants were also best kept at arms' length.

The attendants organized some weekly dances and movies. Mary and I were encouraged to go, and in time were asked, "Why don't you go?" We finally decided to go to one of the dances for a short time.

We slipped in through the rear of the small auditorium around seven o'clock in the evening. The scene was pitiful; a few couples were hanging on to each other as they shuffled around the floor to slow, romantic music. I was told that some of these couples had been "going together" for years. They smiled at each other and held hands when they weren't dancing. These were the ones who bought small gifts for each other at the canteen. There were people sitting around on metal chairs, watching and waiting. They looked like preteen children, hoping that something good would happen to them. Mary and I quickly decided that we had better things to do.

I saw him walk toward me with a swagger, a long scar visible on the right cheek of his large, black face. I remembered seeing him in the canteen. He was about fifty, and he had a reputation for being tough. He must be a chaperone here, I thought. It wasn't until he put his hands on my arm that I realized he wanted to dance with me.

I resisted, and he said, "What's the matter?" I mumbled that attendants weren't supposed to dance with patients. He looked amused and said, "Oh, that's all right. Are you sure you're not trying to say that black attendants aren't supposed to dance with white patients?"

"No, I'm not," I snapped. We were on the floor for the next three dances.

I was walking out when a patient asked me to dance. He was about my height and weight, and he had pale and watery eyes that stared into mine for the entire dance, which was very unnerving. Moreover, his breath was terrible and he was sweating profusely. My first partner was watching with an amused expression on his face. After the dance was over, he said, "Would you like to go with me?" I said, "Yes." He walked away, but he did not return to the canteen and I never saw him again. This was the only dance we attended.

A Murderess

It was during my first month of being in the Women's Building. The two attendants that were working that night were both new to our ward. I had never seen either of them before. The evening was uneventful until it was time to give the night medications. I was taking Dilantin three times a day, as well as a new pill called Librium. After a full work day, I was tired and usually slept well at night. I was next in line and was handed the small cup with my two pills. After she had looked under my tongue to see if they had been swallowed, she handed me a cup of red liquid.

"I don't take that," I said.

"What?" she said angrily.

I told her again that the red liquid was not my medication.

"Well, you do tonight," she spit out. "There's always one." she muttered. "Go sit down." I sat down while she finished the other patients.

She called the other attendant and pointed to some paperwork. They both nodded their heads in agreement. The second attendant walked over to me with the red liquid and shouted, "TAKE IT!"

I don't know what possessed me, but all five-feet-four-inches of me stood up and shouted back, "I will not! It's not mine!"

"Well, well," she said, "you don't shout at us." My hands were pulled behind me in a vise grip. I became frightened as she pulled me down the hall, and I tried to explain. I was shoved into a dark room that had no furniture.

As my eyes adjusted to the dark, something horrified me. I saw a woman crouched in a corner. She was so still that she looked lifeless. There was a blanket on the floor near her. When I realized that her eyes were open and that she was staring at me, I felt paralyzed. I was barefoot and dressed in a thin nightgown, and my body was trembling.

After what seemed like hours, she said, "Do you want to know how I did it?"

I was silent. She moved closer to me and repeated her question.

"Did what?" I whispered.

"With him, he was on the floor, on his back. I put a broomstick across his neck, and then I jumped on it. That neck snapped, clean as a whistle. He was gone. With her, she came around the corner, real sly-like. I waited for her. That knife went in her real easy, just right. It was messy and noisy, but she went out swearing at me for the last time. They hated me all my life, but no more."

I closed my eyes almost completely and didn't say a word. I listened to my own heartbeat. "You, cold?" she asked as she threw the blanket to me. It was a very cold, long night.

The next morning, I heard the door being unlocked. It was Dr. Harkness. She looked very concerned. Her hefty nurse stood at the door. She took off the restraint that was on my wrists and helped me to my feet. I was so stiff that I could hardly stand. I leaned against her nurse until we reached the next room. I answered their questions and was an hour late for work.

The Small Room

After about seven months in the Women's Building, I was moved to a single room. There were two single rooms on this ward, and I was lucky enough to get one of them. It was small - just enough room for a small metal bed and a table with a small drawer. There was a glass window through which any passerby could look in, but it had a door - a door one could close! At night, I could close out all of the noises people made when they slept. It was my very own space.

I began to use my weekly three dollars to buy floor wax. The floor shone, and my little cubicle took on a pleasant scent. The bath schedule was the same, but I felt good about my clean little space. Will visited me weekly now. I showed him where I slept with pride. He seemed pleased, but what could he say? It had to be revolting for him to come to this institution. We went for a walk or sat on the green plastic cushions. Our conversations were not very satisfying. There were the reports about the children, family, neighbors, and the practice of law. We didn't have access to phones at the hospital, so that was the only time for our exchanges. There was rarely anything of interest for me to tell, as I certainly didn't want to burden him any more than I already had. I do remember telling him about my new friends and a few small victories. I did not tell him about my near-rape experience or the many injustices to those who lived there.

When he arrived, the residents stared openly, especially the old women. Who was the handsome young man that arrived in shiny new cars? His business suits were so beautifully tailored. I learned that the condition and style of shoes is very important to downtrodden people, and his always looked special. He walked with confidence, as if he went to important places. "He is *her* husband?" They would shake their heads in wonder and cluck their tongues. "How could that be?" they buzzed to each other. "How could it last?" they asked each other.

My face was taking on the expressions of weariness and sadness. My heart would ache each time he visited me. What would become of us?

Mary

It had been five days since I had seen Mary. She hadn't returned from her leave from the hospital. She had missed the inventory at the Canteen, and Mrs. R. was concerned, too. I knew she had not looked forward to this leave.

I asked Jessie, the day attendant, if she knew anything about Mary's absence. Jessie said she didn't know "nuthin," but she knew Mary didn't want to go. "She never wanted to leave."

"Never?" I questioned.

"You knew she was here for six years before she was committed here?"

"Committed?!" I said in real surprise.

"Oh, yeah. She's thirty-five years old and has spent eight years in mental hospitals."

"Why?" I said in disbelief.

"Well, I think this is a case, clear and simple, of getting rid of someone."

"But she's so steady and reliable. We have become friends."

"What do you know about her?"

"Well, not a lot. She's nice to be around, and I feel like I could have known her from college or an old neighborhood."

"Yeah, I bet," she said as she walked away.

Sonia

Mrs. R. appeared to know no more than I did. Three weeks later, Mrs. R. handed me a newspaper clipping. It read: "MISSING. Local doctor's sister Mary --------- has still not been found. She had not returned from a walk several weeks earlier."

A month later, there was another article: "FOUND. A partially decomposed body of a missing woman was found along a river bank. The woman was the widow of a prominent manufacturer that had preceded her in death ten years earlier of unknown causes. Woman's estate (of some consequence}is willed to a foundation for mentally ill children. Will is in contest by a family member."

My new friend Mary was gone.

Camera Christmas

This is an experience that comes to mind each holiday season. There was a drive in the city that year for the "unfortunate people" in mental hospitals. A plea had gone out, begging people to donate new items for the patients who would not be able to shop for their families. "You can help these people remember their children," one advertisement read. I was one of those fortunate recipients. An aid came to the ward one evening with good news: "Tonight at five, there will be a number of gifts displayed in the recreation room. You may take two gifts for family members. They have been donated, and they can be wrapped by some ladies that are donating their time." Smiles flickered on several faces.

"It'll all be junk nobody wants," someone murmured.

"Come on down and see." As we approached the recreation room, the plastic Santa looked worn and tired. His rosy face looked

The Moving Finger

out of place there, but the tables had wonderful things to offer us. The choices were many - too many for some of us. For some patients, it had been a long time since choices were an issue.

When I saw the small camera, I knew it would be right for Willy. I eagerly picked it up and held it close. I don't remember what the other gift was. There were about eight women that were willing to wrap the gifts in bright paper. They were in their thirties, like me. They looked unbelievably beautiful, clean and fresh, as if they had groomed themselves carefully for this event. A feeling of shame and humility swept over me.

A beautiful blonde woman in a red silk shirt and velvet skirt took my things. Our eyes met. Thank God we did not know each other. My dull and lifeless hair, ragged nails, and ridiculous clothes were humiliating. I saw sympathy in her eyes. "Can I help you?" she said in her cultured Junior League voice. What if she knew that I, too, had been invited to Junior League parties, and that I had been a candidate for membership? She would have laughed in disbelief. I told her the gifts were for my children that I had not seen in six months. I almost whispered this as she chose paper. I did a lot of whispering then. If one whispered, one wasn't seen as clearly. People do that when they are afraid.

A patient began to cry. When I asked her why, she said she couldn't remember her family. "Choose something you like," I suggested. "That helps sometimes." She chose a nice box of soap and had it wrapped in green paper. She left with a smile of satisfaction.

I think that small camera prompted a life-long interest in photography for my son.

The Lilly Ward

It was late in October. The days were getting shorter, and the trees were black silhouettes against the sky without their leaves. I could imagine and visualize people beginning to enjoy their fireplaces. The evidence that growing things were shutting down for awhile contributed to the lack of joy on the hospital grounds. I had shuffled through the leaves on my way back to the Women's Building. The second shift of attendants were leaving for the night.

As I walked through the door, Joanna called my name. "I'm glad you're back early. I have something to tell you." She looked hurried and tired. There was something in her voice that alerted me.

"What?" I asked in a nervous whisper.

"I read in a notice that you're being transferred."

"TRANSFERRED? WHERE?"

With a tight expression around her mouth, she said, "The Lilly Ward."

Something exploded in me and I felt faint. Did I faint? When I became alert again, I was on a low chair, and Joanna was sitting next to me. "I shouldn't have told you, but I was afraid that one of the night girls would tell you and it would catch you off-guard."

"I won't go there!" I said. "I refuse to be a guinea pig for Eli Lilly and Company."

The Moving Finger

The new shift was arriving. "Joanna, will I be able to talk to someone before I'm transferred, or will I be ushered out of here tonight or early tomorrow morning?"

"I don't know. It depends on their mood. I do know that if you are moved in a hurry and the paperwork is done, it would take a while for them to reconsider. Has your husband talked about this with you?"

"No, I haven't seen him for awhile. He's terribly busy. I can see myself ushered out of here with my stuff in a paper bag. Would I have to stop working in the canteen? That's my only therapy."

"Your days would probably be planned differently for awhile." I shuddered. Joanna got up, and with a parting glance, she said, "See ya, honey. Don't worry."

My friend Mary was gone, and who else was there? Betsy was slouched in a green plastic chair. It was rumored that she had been at the hospital for over fifteen years. She and I had slept in the same room when I had first entered this ward. We had exchanged words now and then, but not very many.

"Hi, Betsy. What's new?" I asked in a casual voice.

"Not one goddamn thing! What's new with you, Miss Priss?"

I told her my news. "You don't wanna do that, kid," she said in a loud voice.

"Were you ever there?" I asked.

"Yes, I was there, and it screwed me up terrible. You'll probably leave early in the morning when things are real calm around here."

Sonia

"Sure, real calm," I said. "They can't do this to me," I said with false bravado.

"OHH, yes they can! Any time they please or anywhere they want. You got a husband. He ought to know about it."

"Yes, I do, but I don't think he knows."

"He must have given them permission."

"I've always gone voluntarily, but not this."

"Do you have any money?" she whispered.

"Three dollars."

"I have an idea for preventing a quick shoo-out, so you can at least talk to Dr. Harkness in the morning when she comes in. Two floors up are the demented folks. They lay all over the place, sleep, and rock in a stupor. If you put your blanket over your head like a shawl, mess up your hair, put on those old glasses, some socks, and drip that juice over there down your front, you'd fit right in."

"What?" I gasped in shock.

"Well, they sure as hell wouldn't find you in the morning now, would they? The girls that work up there play cards, talk, or do their nails. The only thing that gets their attention is fighting, screaming, or someone on the floor. Just go in casual-like and go lay down. If someone asks you something, just go dumb. Don't say a word. There's a big turnover in the night girls."

I looked doubtful as I went to prepare, but I asked, "What's the Lilly Ward like, Betsy?"

"Well, let's put it this way - someone doesn't think you're coming along like you should."

"Someone?"

"Who knows? Lilly and other pill companies are looking for big breakthroughs in treating mental illness. One good drug can carry them for years. You're here 'cause you are sick. It's a state hospital. The hospital and the pill companies have an arrangement where experimental drugs can be used on the ward that they pay for. Some drugs could help, or they can really screw you up."

It was getting late. I would do what Betsy had suggested and see Dr. H. in the morning. I asked Riva, a roommate, to stuff my bed so it looked like I was there sleeping.

My feet dragged as I went up the stairs where I had never been. I cautiously slipped past the small group at the door. That was lucky, I thought, as I tried to control a large gasp; I didn't know it was a locked ward. These women must wander off and get lost.

I aimed for a green plastic cushion with my head down and my fingers working the blanket nervously. The smell of unwashed bodies was terrible. It was hard to keep from retching. I could hear a chair rocking nearby. Looking up slowly, I saw a toothless old woman grinning, but otherwise she showed little sign of life. I thought of bolting out of there, but decided against it - it would be just for one night. Someone was moaning, as if they were in pain. Across the room, the sound of strange laughter echoed. The woman next to me screamed as someone touched her arm. An aide sauntered over to her side. Someone was studying me. I saw white shoes through the slits of my eyes.

"What are you doing here?" the voice asked. I slowly looked up into two large brown eyes and gazed into them vacantly without a word, drooling a little as my fingers worked the blanket.

She shrugged her shoulders and walked away. Someone called, "Medicine, ladies!" I went to the water fountain for a drink of the warm and stale water, then I turned into a dormitory. I lay down on a bed far from the door and light. People began wandering in and taking a bed. Were the beds assigned? Surely they must be, but apparently no one wanted the bed that I had taken.

One woman walked over to me, studied me for a minute, shook her head, and took the next bed. During a quick trip to the ancient bathroom, I noticed several women sleeping on the green plastic sofas. They each had one of the small gray blankets over them. The attendants were napping, doing paperwork, or talking. They had not noticed the younger, very thin woman in their midst. My disguise had been good. I thought sadly about these inmates. They had been rejected by their families and by the system. They would live and die in this warehouse for the mentally ill. I thought to myself that if only the people who were kind and giving knew the plight of these poor forgotten women, maybe they would share some of the things they enjoyed. However, I knew that these women were a well-kept secret.

A Walk to Ayres

The traffic was sporadic. There were drivers in a hurry, and others were just out cruising. The hesitant drivers that appeared lost were probably confused. The medical center where the hospital was located consisted of many buildings, and there were few signs. The road along which I was walking was as straight as an arrow. It was daring of me to walk several miles alone. No one would notice

The Moving Finger

me, I told myself. If they did, it would be obvious that I was carrying nothing of interest, not even a purse. My shabby skirt and blouse were ill-fitting and faded. My shoes had lost their shape and were run down at the heels. Due to early ballet training and a lifelong habit, my posture was good and my movement was somewhat graceful, which pleased me as I walked down the littered street.

It was a Saturday in September. The air was fresh and balmy. It was surprising that, despite limited diet and being underweight, I could walk the distance fairly easily, which was almost two miles each way, but nonetheless slowly. It took a lot of courage that first time - I had become so fearful.

Walking alone to the middle of the city didn't bother me that day, not even through the industrial areas with their abandoned buildings. The occasional unsavory-looking pedestrian seemed less threatening than at any other time of my life.

Working in the canteen had begun to change my life. I could walk away from the hospital grounds and through the intimidating gates, and it was becoming a challenge to see how far I could go. Maybe I should have told someone I was going so far that day. Who would I tell? I asked myself. There was a drugstore several blocks away from which I bought things occasionally. Being allowed $3.00 a week from family added up: I had $11.00 in my pocket, which to me was a small fortune. I had put an old driver's license in my pocket as an afterthought; some identity seemed as though it could be helpful.

What had motivated me to go downtown was an item in the newspaper ads: "Panties 2 for $1.00 and bras for $3.00." Over time, my things had become ill-fitting and dingy. Washing them in the rusty bucket with the strong soap had taken its toll. I had opened a charge account at L.S. Ayres as a single working girl almost ten years prior.

THE CAR WAS SLOWING DOWN. The man's face and long stringy blonde hair scared me. The two men in the backseat were laughing as our eyes met. Their language was getting rough, and they were arguing. The driver accelerated quickly, and rubber squealed on the pavement. It was then that I noticed the police car. It pulled up alongside me.

"Where are you going?" asked the policeman in a kind voice.

"To L. S. Ayres, the department store," I said as pertly as I could.

"Where are you from?"

With just a slight hesitancy in my voice, I said, "Oh, I work in one of the buildings at the medical center."

"Hmm. Well, take care now, ya hear?" My head rocked up and down in agreement.

The store was only four blocks away - at last.

I forgot how out of place I would be. As I looked around, everyone looked so well-groomed and confident. They were moving with purpose. They would do their shopping and meet friends for lunch in the celebrated Tea Room. One beautiful family had an appointment with a photographer. My eyes stung with hot tears. "None of that," I told myself sternly. I have a purpose here, too.

The basement was crowded with people like me. We were looking for the least expensive items. I was happy to be one of them. I saw what I came for. They were crudely made, and the fabrics were stiff and coarse; but they would fit, I told myself gratefully, and they were new. My spirits soared: my $11.00 was enough.

The walk back was long but rewarding. Holding the crisp new paper bag with my new items made my steps lighter. I had made another huge step in my recovery.

On Home Leave

After a few months at Central State, I was allowed to go home for a day at a time to be with my family. I was deliriously happy at first, but then fear began to creep into my mind. Going home from the hospital for short visits or overnight was really frightening. It would seem as if those would be precious times to anticipate and enjoy. It was only natural that someone had to come in and take over in my absence. It was a busy home with three young active boys. We were fortunate that Will's mother lived nearby and was able to manage the house and the family. She adored her eldest son and our children. One Sunday morning, Will came to take me home for a visit. I dreaded seeing the masked look of distaste when he saw me. He seemed so out of place when he came to pick me up. He was handsome and fresh in his poplin J. Press suit, beautiful light blue oxford cloth shirt, and pricey, well-shined loafers. He gave me a light hug in greeting, and I pulled back a little so I would not soil or wrinkle his clothing. This was the same man who had pleaded with me to go out with him when we were young. He led me to the new, navy blue Oldsmobile that I had never ridden in. It smelled new and clean, and it was so big! As we went out the gate, I had no feelings of elation; I was afraid. I hadn't been warned that this would be another huge adjustment. I didn't know that it would be so destructive to go home and pretend that things were the same as they had always been. I hadn't seen my children for months. It was decided between Will and his mother that the children shouldn't see me in "that place," although I did believe that my children could have been brought to the canteen for a brief visit. At least they would have known that I wasn't locked up or strapped down.

As I walked into the house, I wondered what I should do or say. What if I saw a neighbor or friend? What would they want to know? How could I explain? What if one of my children's friends came over to play? Would they be embarrassed for some reason?

At this point, a counselor would have been invaluable. I had the hospital and the medicine, but no one to talk to. When I came home for weekends, I didn't know what was expected of me. I remember working on the dandelions in the front yard with great energy. We would go to church as a family, but I often left in a panic, leaving my family to wonder what was going on and why I left. There are no words that I can find to do justice in explaining the fear and the panic that was with me for so long. It is something I never experience now. Was it the medication? My illness? I have never been given an answer to what ravaged me and my dear family for so long. Will and I didn't talk about our fears. Our worlds were too different. I would tell my friends how good and loyal Will was to me.

The Moving Finger

How lonely and discouraging having a wife in a mental hospital with no end in sight must have been for him.

What was my role now? Was there an advantage to anyone because I was home? If only we could talk to each other freely - but we couldn't. It seemed as if my education in teaching and his education in law would have contributed to our skills in communication, but this was a very emotional thing for us to discuss, and psychiatry had not been a part of our formal education.

I was home on very short visits. In a way, I felt like a guest, and there were no advantages to pretending that I was a full-time occupant. Taking charge and organizing the home to my liking only made it harder for the full-time homemaker after I left. My visits were very bittersweet experiences. We were all in uncharted waters.

We began our lives together with so much confidence, love, and dreams. We didn't know how to get back there. We had taken our wedding vows seriously when we were married, and we assumed that they would last forever. In my heart, I assumed that there would be nothing that we couldn't survive together. I hoped that we could overcome those terrible circumstances that were no fault of our own.

However, the visits became more strained and unsatisfying for both of us. At this point, it would have been valuable to have a third person (not a psychiatrist) counsel us. We might have had a better chance, or maybe we would have always been reminded of this sad and overwhelming chapter in our lives.

Eventually, Will withdrew from me physically. He didn't want me anymore. I began to think there was someone else in his life and in his bed. He was drinking more. I never judged him for this, but I worried that he would go to bars and meet the wrong people, lonely people who would be only too willing to fill his empty hours.

My family wasn't really mine anymore from that point on. I had lost the dream of my life with a healthy, loving, and thriving family. How I resented that I was only thirty-five years old, and the roles of being a wife, mother, and homemaker were essentially gone. How cheated we all were. It felt like I was an intruder in my family's life. The relaxed and joyous banter of ordinary families was gone for us.

Eventually, I went home for several days. I can remember awakening in the night. I was tense, panicked, and wet with perspiration. The children were sleeping in the next room, and I was afraid of waking up anyone since Will had a trial the next day. What would take this scary thing away? I had to conceal this feeling of panic. I was home and safe. There was no hysterical screaming now, and there weren't any rats the size of cats lurking in the corners. No stranger would touch me in the dark here.

Trying to pretend that these fearful times didn't happen while I was home made them worse.

"You aren't ready to go home," I was told.

"How do you get ready?" I would fearfully ask.

Finally, I was summoned before the same group who had examined me after my admission to Central State. They said I was being released to go home.

Press Clippings (BOX)

The Indiana Hospital for the Insane, renamed Central State Hospital in 1929, closed its doors for good in 1994.

Anna Agnew's exposé of conditions at the institution, written after her discharge in 1885, were not the last. Over the years, the hospital received its fair share of attention from the media for alleged abuses, including the death of some patients. This contributed to Governor Evan Bayh's decision to close the facility.

Central State opened its doors in 1848. Thirty years later, the Women's Building was ready for use. The building had more than one thousand rooms and sixty-five miles of steam lines to furnish heat.

One of Anna's most vocal complaints after her discharge was that the public should not be allowed to visit the hospital and observe the behavior of the insane as a form of entertainment. Hordes of people were coming since the street car was routed in from of the hospital.

TRACES, Indiana Historical Society, Spring 2001.

The city's $450,000 purchase of Central State Hospital, a former mental institution, will go through despite evidence of marked graves in at least two locations. The graves could affect which portions of the 146-acre property are developed and which are left alone.

Indianapolis Star, September 2003

5. Attempted Suicide

To My Sons

There are times when I can hardly believe the poignancy of my illness. It seems unbelievable that I tried to take my own life. I am the one who carries bugs outdoors to avoid killing them. I have enjoyed nursing sick plants back to health. As a little girl, I couldn't understand how people could enjoy stomping on ants and other living things for no reason. I respected all life.

In March of 1972, I attempted suicide. It was the only time that I took such a desperate action. As I look back to that time (which I rarely do), it is hard for me to believe that I could not conceive then of an alternative solution. I was a source of embarrassment for all of you, my sons, and I am sorry about that. Did all of this leave awful scars?

Why did the return to my beloved family after the pure hell of Central State lead me, to wanting to end my life? I can only sense some of the reasons. Central State, although traumatic, was also extremely structured. I had practically nothing to worry about while

I was there, and I had to focus all of my efforts on survival. When I returned home, my choices were many and difficult. The many years of illness and stays in mental hospitals had changed me in ways that are difficult to describe. I had more fear, which sometimes led to panic. I needed more time to myself, but also to communicate complex feelings and concerns. Will, too, had changed through my long illness and absences. Unfortunately, we were unable to talk to each other about these experiences, thoughts, and feelings. Everyone around me tried to act as if nothing had happened, as if we could resume a normal life as a family, but it took a long time for my many wounds to heal enough for that to happen. I did not feel that I could live up to expectations, especially mine, of what a good wife and mother should be and do. This frustration put unbelievable pressure on me, which grew to the point that removing myself finally from the scene seemed like the only way out of the box.

Fatigue was my worst enemy. If I had had the energy to cook, clean, and do the other things that I expected of myself, I might have felt better. I felt guilty having my family eat "carry-ins." Will worked hard every day and deserved better than stopping after work to buy that night's meal, which unfortunately happened more frequently as time passed. If I really tried, a meal should not have been too much for me to prepare, but it was.

The cost of my doctors and hospitals must have been staggering for a young attorney. No one in my family neglected me, and everyone was very kind to me.

As far as I was concerned, if I wasn't there, so many problems would have been solved immediately. My death would free us all. It wasn't that I didn't love you or think you weren't the most beautiful and wonderful children in the world; as I saw it, a new life was waiting for you. Your handsome, intelligent, fine father would marry again in time. Trips to the zoo and picnics in the park could be yours again. How could I stand in the way of happiness for you and in the way of peace for me?

The Attempt

I was unwilling to end my life by drowning or jumping. I began to save pills and filled two bottles, thinking that I might need them sometime. I had stopped calling most of my old friends. What was there to say? Our good friends Sarah and Jack kept inviting us to parties. Sometimes I went, too, no matter how self conscious I felt. I will always be grateful to them for inviting us. They cared and they tried. To me, the women were all beautiful, witty, interesting, and normal, and I self-consciously magnified the meaning of their occasionally questioning glances.

It was a cool fall day, and the house was quiet. Everyone was gone and would be away for hours. I remember very vividly walking into the bathroom and seeing my face in the mirror. I stepped closer to the mirror so I could look into my eyes deeply. For some reason, my vision was more distorted than usual, as if I was looking through a sheer fabric. The pupils of my eyes were huge. I made up my mind to take my life.

It was early in the day, which would be time enough for my body to be removed before my children came home from school. Sadly, I thought, Florence will find me. At first, she would weep, but then she would be free to live her own life. She worked much too hard doing the work that I should be doing. My husband might grieve some, but he would become a free man. He deserved more than what he had now. I thought my father would understand, but I could not bear to think about my mother. Get on with it, I thought!

I swallowed the bottles of pills, and then I drank a helping of Scotch Whiskey. With a very sharp knife, I sliced the very large veins on both hands. There was no slashing of my wrists or gouging; just deep cuts through the veins. I asked God for forgiveness and lay back on the bed.. I felt very calm but sorrowful. I had made the best attempt I knew how to make while still avoiding any possible publicity. My family had suffered enough.

Having survived a near death, I felt no joy or relief when I awakened in the hospital. The problem was still there, and the situation was worse. But then I began a long-overdue healing process.

The letter I received from my father after this attempt was no surprise to me. He was a very resourceful man who understood a great deal and helped me to think in a much more positive way about my life.

Letter from My Father

The following letter and philosophy reshaped my thinking for the years to come. I received it shortly after my suicide attempt.

Walloon Lake - March 4, 1972

My Ever Dear Sonia,

It seems to me that you are entitled to know exactly how I feel about your recent experience. In any event, I am going to tell you, simply because my personal philosophy has worked fairly well for me over a considerable period of time.

I have the happy faculty of turning the page and never rereading the past:

"THE MOVING FINGER HAVING WRIT,

MOVES ON, NOR ALL THY PIETY, NOR ALL THY WIT,

SHALL CANCEL HALF A LINE OF IT."

--Omar Khayyam, Persia, 4th Century AD

To me, the past is past, and it interests me not at all.

Fortunately for me and my peace of mind, your recent incident is over and done with. I shall not refer to it again for the simple reason that I shall not think of it. It is out of my mind now and in the future.

I have told you many times that it is the future that counts, not the past. This is what I want to write about in this letter.

I have thought from time to time that you are underestimating yourself and your importance to us all. You know, or should know, how dear you are to Will, your children, and to your mother, brother, and your father. What you may underestimate is your great importance to all of us in the days, months and years to come. The mother is the very center and keystone of the family. You have a fine husband and precious children. They need you above all else. Your parents need you and take the greatest comfort from your well-being, and on the other hand, we suffer most of all when you are not well in body and spirit. In my way of thinking, you just can't write yourself off as being less than of total importance to each and every one of us, each in his or her own way.

So much, my dear, for this day's philosophy. The matter is closed. We open a new chapter. I look to tomorrow, next week, and next year with perfect hope and expectations.

Wait until you see your Uncle Frank's portrait. It covers most of the fireplace chimney in the dining room, just like Figaro's nose. Another thing: don't forget that this is the year someone needs to paint the dock, and that someone is little old you. We plan to see you and your family soon, but above all, your precious self.

I send my love and remain as you well know,

Your Devoted Father

6. Separation and Divorce

Frictions in Our Marriage

I had attempted suicide, and it was shocking to me that I had survived. Florence had come home early and found me unconscious. The ambulance pulled away as my children returned from school. It had been a selfish act, and it had created more pain and uncertainty for my family. I never knew how my children reacted to this act of mine, or even what they were told. I have never discussed these events with them, and they have never raised the issue with me.

When I returned home from the emergency room, I slowly began to arrange household items to my liking. I also began to establish a routine. I spent as much time as I could in the yard, taking on the dandelions with great energy. I prepared simple meals, kept clothes clean, and chased the dust around and around. I began to walk our dog, Hess, but at first I was afraid to go far. That seemed strange considering my long walks from the hospital in dangerous neighborhoods. When we walked around the block,

The Moving Finger

I put my outdated driver's license in my pocket in the event that I might need identification.

I became more involved in the lives of my children, becoming a "room mother" in their school, communicating with their teachers, and selling hot dogs at Little League games. During that first week, I went to see my psychiatrist for the last time. There was a different atmosphere during this visit. He remained distant and almost stern. I have no memory of what was said.

It wasn't long before I knew that Will was abusing alcohol. He had grown up in a home where alcohol wasn't allowed. His Quaker and Baptist upbringing had forbidden it. At school, he went overboard, and beer was around on every occasion. My parents were annoyed at how many beer cans were left on the beach and in the beach house during our frequent visits. I had always excused this with, "It's vacation time," or, "It's a party. He needs to let off steam and relax."

In our early years, I ignored his overindulgence. He was never abusive and never created scenes. I would only teasingly warn him. During his years in the Air Force, he was very careful. After that, however, he began playing games, especially on weekends and vacations. There were open cans of beer hidden in closets, the basement, the garage, the bedroom, in our cars, and even in bushes. Thinking that this was not observable, he was "making the rounds" all day. Eventually, his speech would become slurred and he would say and do foolish things.

In the newspaper, I read a notice about a group called Al-Anon that would be meeting during the following week. I had not driven a car for several years and was not anxious to begin again, but the notice appealed to me, and I made the decision to drive the two miles despite Will's objections. I can remember how timidly I got into the car and turned on the ignition. I drove slowly and cautiously, my heart racing. Upon arriving, I became very concerned that someone would recognize me, which could be destructive to Will's reputation. Feeling I had done enough damage already, I returned home.

Later that week, Will and I went out to dinner alone for a celebration of some kind. I could smell beer on his breath before we left. We waited a long time for our food to arrive at the restaurant, during which we had several drinks. Before we were served, I was shocked to see how unsteadily Will walked to and from the men's room. I said I was going to the ladies' room, but instead I called our oldest son. I asked him to drive to the restaurant and wait outside until we exited, and I explained that we needed a ride home. Will became angry and insulting to the waitress, saying that the food was too late. He threw fifty dollars on the table. "That should do it," he said in slurred speech and stormed out the door. I told him our son was on his way to give us a ride home. He told me to "GET IN THE CAR," which I refused to do. He drove home alone, and I rode with our son.

The next week, I went to the Al-Anon meeting and became a member for the next ten years. At first, I excused and sympathized with Will's need for alcohol. I told myself that he had been alone so much and that his burdens had been overwhelming, but he had become argumentative and began to take chances when under the influence.

After several meetings at Al-Anon, I knew I belonged there. The group consisted of articulate and sensitive people who were searching for peace and serenity in their lives and looked forward, not backwards. After a few meetings, I began to feel accepted for who I was, and I began to gain self-confidence.

The meetings were for the families of alcoholics. Only first names were used, and criticism, placing blame, or getting revenge were not accepted. The twelve steps of AA's wonderful book <u>One Day At A Time</u> set the topics for thought and discussion. Al-Anon taught me a way of thinking that saved my life. I learned to live one day at a time, sometimes one hour at a time. I learned to accept things I could not change and to have the courage to change the things I could. Finding the wisdom to know the difference between what I could and could not change took a long time and a lot of prayer. Above all, I learned that I had the right to free myself from a situation that prevented me from having a decent life.

Will and I never went out to dinner again. An unyielding barrier of silence and resentment grew between us. We were no longer lovers or even friends.

Frustrations

In the early days of our marriage, Will and I were like magnets. After our marriage was over, I realized that there was plenty of quantity - but not much quality - in our lovemaking. There was no doubt that we loved each other and had fun as we reveled in each other's young and beautiful bodies, but we were inexperienced and uneducated about sex.

In high school, I was not one of the girls that people looked at slyly and whispered, "She does it." I had a steady boyfriend with whom I did a great deal of sexual exploration, but we always stopped short of intercourse. We "parked" along country lanes, hugging and kissing up a storm; we reached climaxes with our clothes on. I didn't know what to call that wonderful feeling down there, or even that it had a name, and we certainly didn't talk about it - we just enjoyed it.

After marriage, when sex became legal, blessed, and expected, all of this changed. I became increasingly frustrated about *something* that I couldn't name. I certainly couldn't say, "Let's go park on a country lane, leave our clothes on, and hug and kiss up a storm," when we had a bedroom in which we could be naked on a large bed with privacy. I could hardly say, "I'm not getting that wonderful, exciting feeling down there that I got when I "parked" with my high school boyfriend."

When I became really frustrated, my feelings and thoughts were not taken seriously or addressed with tenderness. After two years, I clumsily told my gynecologist that I had a problem. He was very understanding and filled in the proper words and expressions for me. He believed that, with a little patience and time, there should be no problem. He gave me a small book that we discussed. He said, "Give this to your husband to look over. Remember, time and patience."

I felt stricken - Will didn't like to have his manhood questioned, and a "how to" book could really irritate him. I had seen his reactions on other subjects in the past, but why should I be denied this pleasure? I remember agonizing over the right time to give him the book. One day after fixing a nice dinner, I saw Will was relaxed after several beers. Tempting smells wafted from the kitchen, and we hadn't had sex for two days. After we had finished dinner, we went to our favorite seats to read or chat. I held my breath and smiled as I handed him the book. He looked at the cover and then inside briefly. I breathed a sigh of relief; the hard part was over. Then he threw the book on the floor and said in real anger, "I don't need any goddamn book." This was the end of the matter, except for brooding.

I was terribly disappointed. Maybe I shouldn't have smiled, or maybe the timing was wrong. We never discussed this subject again. I comforted myself with, "Maybe that's the way it is with most people," but what a small comfort that was!

Thirty one years, five pregnancies, and three children later, I left my husband and moved into an apartment. I made an acquaintance at the Methodist church nearby, where classes and lectures were offered for women who had separated from their husbands. We were in several classes together and sometimes met for dinner. One day, my new friend handed me a package. "This will help," she said with her big toothy grin. Enclosed was a book written for women about sex. There was also an object shaped like a man's penis. I was truly shocked and embarrassed; I'm sure my face was scarlet. She laughed heartily at my expression and then said, "Read the book. You'll know what to do." Also enclosed was the magazine

New Woman, with a note: "That magazine is a life saver and will become a best friend." I became a liberated woman. Never had a gift changed my life like this one.

Separation

The tension between us continued to grow. Will's weight was ballooning, and his face had an unhealthy flush. He was not overtly unkind; he just withdrew from me. We were like strangers in the same house. His life did not include me any longer.

Intellectually, I can understand how this could have happened over time. Emotionally, it was destructive to both of us.

One evening, Will and I went to a dinner and dance sponsored by Will's firm. I dressed for the occasion, wearing a long black Halston dress with a matching scarf and the diamonds my Aunt Nell had left me. My long, dark hair was pulled up in a chignon, and I wore light makeup but accentuated my blue eyes, dark lashes, and brows. Will's associates were very appreciative and openly admiring. But that night, Will was distracted as we made love. I knew, as only a woman can, that he was having an affair.

The year before, I had flown to Petoskey, Michigan, to visit with my mother who was ill with cancer. Our family was there for her last Christmas. It was the last time my children or husband saw their greatest champion - she loved them dearly. Again that year, I flew back and went with her to a Traverse City hospital for chemotherapy.

I was there when she died, and I was grateful that she didn't know about our new problems. After her death, Will and I both inherited $10,000 from her. She had sold her rental properties in the village of Walloon Lake and divided the profit between us and her husband.

We decided to put in a new kitchen, air conditioner, and carpet into the first home we owned. It looked lovely, and it was a good project for Will and me to work on together. However, the children would soon be in high school, and we were concerned about the choices of schools in our school district. I began to look at homes further north, where the schools were better.

A friend called one day with the good news that a house I was interested in was going on the market, and it was not yet in the hands of a realtor. I met with the owner, and she walked me through the one-story ranch home on a glorious lot in an upscale neighborhood.

"How much does it cost?" I asked boldly.

With no hesitation, she said, $100,000."

I countered with, "How about $75,000?"

"That's good. I'll accept that."

I could hardly believe our good fortune. This neighborhood had easy access to the best high schools in the city. I called Will and told him the good news, and he said he would look at this house.

We had bought our first house for $25,000, and we sold it for $50,000. We agreed on buying the house further north. There were a few problems with the new house, but it was livable and we enjoyed our new surroundings. We had some lovely and festive holiday meals there, which I prepared with pride. I also had a great sense of relief about the progress that I had made. It was good to have the family together again, and Will's mother was always supportive and helpful in my efforts. She had her own apartment back in her hometown that was near friends and family.

In spite of these achievements, nothing had really changed between us. I had heard that Will was having an affair with an acquaintance of one of my oldest and best friends. During a weekend visit to Walloon Lake to see the children and me, he took a foolish risk. Will's lover and her husband were visiting my friend and her family at their cottage across the lake. While we were sleeping, Will went down to the dock alone with a telescope and turned the boat house lights on and off as a signal. Simultaneously, my friend observed his lover (her guest) gyrating on her dock directly across the lake. Evidently, they were giving each other intimate messages at an appointed time. I did not learn about this until several years later after our divorce had become final, when he finally admitted that this relationship had been of long standing and that he had previously had several other affairs.

I had come a long way since my attempted suicide. I had not seen a psychiatrist or been hospitalized for two years. I was driving cautiously and attending Al-Anon meetings faithfully. I began substitute teaching at a neighborhood school. The principal and teachers liked me, and I was called often. It seemed as though I became less awkward as I wove around the students' desks while they worked on assignments. The principal asked if I would like to become a permanent substitute teacher for the rest of the year and a candidate for a regular teaching job. I was greatly pleased, but I could not become eligible for a regular teaching job in the public schools until I had completed a master's degree in education. At that time, I decided to resume my studies. I had returned to the mainstream of life.

Living together with Will had become intolerable. The two older boys were in high school, and the youngest had only two years of grade school left. After considerable thought, I told Will I wanted a legal separation.

He didn't disagree. His response was, "I'm not going anywhere."

Leaving home and striking out alone was scary. I had no money and no permanent job. I would lose the health insurance from Will's firm. The car that I would use was old and beat-up. My vision problems would never correct themselves. And what if I had seizures on the street, in the car, or on the job and ended up in another institution?

I had my Al-Anon friends, and they were the only group that I was comfortable with. I had made one special friend named Barbara, who became my Al-Anon sponsor. Over time, I had told her only part of my personal concerns. On a lovely spring day, I made a decision. I asked Barbara to meet me at an apartment complex. I showed her a small available apartment that I liked. She agreed hesitantly and with no enthusiasm that it was a nice apartment. We went to the office, and I made out two checks - one for a month's rent and the other for a deposit. My father had agreed to lend me a little money; he trusted me.

As we left, Barbara said, " I'm shocked you would do this." She had no idea that my plan was to separate legally from my husband,

and perhaps to divorce him. Al-Anon was not the place where these issues were discussed or where anyone was encouraged to take such measures. Yet I knew that she didn't disapprove completely.

With the help of my children, I took furniture and other things out of the house that had been my mother's and grandmother's. This small apartment became my home and refuge. I made it as homey as possible with my familiar things. This move had to be successful.

I thought about the scared rabbit that I had been, afraid of everything and so uncertain. No one could ignore me here, and no one could scream obscenities at me. I would not ruminate about why I was being mistreated.

The day that I finished moving, I closed the door, sat on my one chair, and took a very deep breath. Then I went through the motions of making things as orderly as possible in the kitchen and bedroom. I remember so vividly making my single bed with crisp white sheets that had a piece of cheap lace at the top. The pillow slip matched the sheets.

I also had a white lightweight comforter that was fresh and comfortable. It was getting dark, which made me wonder about how that first night would be when I was totally on my own for the first time. The traffic from the street was faint and, for some reason, comforting. I had just left my husband (who at one time had been my best friend and lover), my confused children, and my sweet old dog named Hess.

Before going to bed, I took a long, warm bath and slipped into my small bed. I said a prayer of hope and praise. That first night,

I slept uninterrupted for twelve wonderful hours. It had been a long time since I had slept so peacefully.

The next day, I went to the grocery store for a few food items and a newspaper. I no longer had valid credit cards, and there was only $178 in my checking account. I needed a job immediately. With a yellow marker, I circled practically all of the ads for jobs that I could conceivably qualify for. I couldn't go back to teaching full-time until I received a master's degree. It had been seventeen years since I was in school, and it had been almost that long since I had been in the job market. It would be tough. Hot weather was beginning, and I thought of my friends going to their summer homes with their families. There would be no vacations for me for a long time, and I didn't really care at this point - I had an agenda.

As a start that first summer, I took a part-time minimum wage job at a daycare center near my apartment. Taking care of small children was a joy for me. The old car that my children called "Ole Blue" was a new source of confidence-building. There were some "fender benders," but they weren't serious. They were not always my fault, and no one was ever hurt.

I had a number of interviews for low paying full-time jobs, but I was often rejected for being "overqualified." A college degree in education apparently turned them off; if they had only known how willing I was to do their menial tasks! In the fall, I tried working as a desk person at a dry cleaner. This was a disaster - customers were hurried and impatient. I was too slow and got very confused with their bookkeeping system, and I was soon told to look elsewhere, which was very humiliating. I was a replacement for a few months in the classified section of a small newspaper, which was very enjoyable. Babysitting for a friend while she worked and substitute teaching also added slightly to my income.

Preparing for Divorce

Having left my husband and living independently, I knew that a divorce was highly likely. I planned to wait until my children were in high school or beyond. The Al-Anon meetings that I had been attending regularly were good therapy for me. They gave me a support group in which I felt comfortable, and I was gaining in confidence.

I had taken my first step by seeking the opinion of my doctor, a friend of the former psychiatrist with whom I had a good relationship, during an annual physical exam. He was a soft-spoken and conservative family man with an excellent reputation. I told him of my plans to start divorce proceedings. I was shocked but encouraged by his answer: "Do it. This marriage is killing you."

At some point, I received this letter from him: "It was a real pleasure to see you in the office on December 11, 1979. Prior health problems have included: anxiety problems, disease of the breast, tension headaches, spastic colon, and trochanteric bursitis. Prior medicines include Tyrane, Sinequan, unprocessed bran, Dilantin, and Tylenol. Current complaints include occasional headaches, slightly irregular menses, premenstrual tension, and tenderness in the left hip when you lie on it. Lab results - Normal.

"We recommend that you continue your present, active life. I am so tickled that you have found your work on a master's

The Moving Finger

degree to be so challenging and interesting. I am in total accord with you slowly trying to wean yourself down from the tranquilizers and antidepressants that you have been using. It sounds to me like you have your act together. I found nothing in your Physical examination to suggest significant disease."

At about the same time, I also consulted a priest in my parish. This took a lot of courage, considering what I wanted to talk about. There had been a divorce in my family, but it wasn't ever discussed. If divorce became an issue, where would I stand in my beloved church?

The priest was pleasant and kind after I presented a rather vague account of my marriage. In essence, the conversation went as follows:

"Since your husband is not a Roman Catholic, there are conditions where an annulment can be requested."

"But we have three children, and they were conceived in marriage."

He looked weary as he said, "Go home, sit on your husband's lap, and love him up."

I thanked him and left. During Lent that year, I went to mass every day looking for wisdom, or even for a sign.

The hardest part was telling my sons about the divorce. Their replies astonished me. My oldest son's response was, "You should have done it a long time ago." The second one's answer was, "I don't know what else you can do." I don't remember a response from my youngest son. I had no idea any of them would volunteer a response.

I told myself that surely it can't be wrong when being together is so destructive. There was no relationship left, physically or mentally. We had been through so much pain. We avoided each other in different ways. When we came together infrequently, it was in sadness and with accusations. We no longer blamed fate or bad luck; we blamed each other. Now I knew for certain that there were other women. One of my sons had begun meeting them and their children, and he told me so.

My greatest concern now was the attitude of the Catholic Church. I loved my church, and my Irish Catholic upbringing was strong. Could I justify divorce? Well, I did.

The one thing that shook my reasoning was the opinion of some old friends from law school. "Aren't you being a bit too ungrateful by doing this? Your husband has stayed with you and supported you over some pretty difficult years." Yes, I would nod my head sadly, but I felt no obligation to explain this move. My few close friends needed no explanation. "Be grateful for what he did for you," some would say. I was grateful for some things, but not a lot. He had left me long before I moved out. It was up to me to do the dirty work of initiating a divorce. Where would I find the strength and determination? I came to the conclusion that survival is a strong instinct.

Finding a lawyer was hard. Two of my friends refused to represent me, explaining that this was not their field of expertise. I decided to find the most experienced and successful divorce lawyer that I could find on my own. He was used to high profile cases that were worth a lot of money, but ours wouldn't be like that.

The entire process took over two years, which was hard. I was living alone in an apartment and working at the best minimum wage jobs that I could find. When Thanksgiving and Christmas came around, I was alone. That was painful and understandable, since I was the one who left. There was a Methodist church near where I lived. They had a study group of women, several of whom were alone with their children. They invited me to share their celebrations.

It was so odd - I had longed to be with my family on these days when I couldn't, and now we were separated by choice. At this point, it was probably a relief that we weren't in the same house.

I was glad my mother didn't witness these proceedings. It would have been another source of disappointment for her. She loved my husband. He had become like a son to her. They even resembled each other. She was proud of his handsome good looks and his success in practicing law. Before we were married, she asked me, "How will your intended earn a living?"

I replied confidently, "Oh, after the Air Force, he's going to law school."

"What if he doesn't go on to school?" she asked.

"Oh, he will. It's part of our plan," I said.

It was somewhat different with my father. There were things that he liked about my intended husband, but I was his only daughter. Was there anyone good enough? Apparently so, because they eventually became business partners. My dad paid most of the bills during our three years in Bloomington with the understanding that he would eventually be paid back. Time spent in the Air Force Reserves paid the rest. Those were the only two sources of income that the five of us had at that time. There were some huge differences between the two men in my life, but they never became an issue and did not interfere with their friendship and trust in each other.

I'm not sure why, but my father always trusted my judgment. When I told him that I was divorcing my husband, he was disappointed, but he said, "I will do what I can to help you, but understand, I'm not a wealthy man. I've planned carefully for my remaining years, but we'll manage." My heart overflowed in gratitude.

I later made one final effort to find out whether my marriage to Will could be salvaged. I invited Will to come to my apartment; we had had little contact since the separation. We discussed the children, however unsatisfactorily. I asked him why he had not sent me the $900 a month that our agreement stipulated for several months. With sad and downcast eyes, he replied, "I can't afford it." I did not argue, reaffirming my independence. After a beer or two, I enticed him into the bedroom, trying one final time to see how things would evolve. I wanted to find out whether the old magnetism was truly dead. Nothing developed; neither of us really wanted a sexual encounter. I knew exactly where I stood and could go forward without looking back. My hospital friend, Mary, would approve. I called my lawyer to begin divorce proceedings.

Divorce Proceedings

On the day that my husband and I were to appear before the judge for a divorce settlement, I called my good friend, Barbara, from Al-Anon. She agreed to go with me. She drove me to my lawyer's office, which was only a short walk from the courthouse.

My lawyer, J., met me with an outstretched hand. "Are you ready?"

"I hope so," I whispered.

"We'll be in chambers in twenty minutes. Remember, answer only the questions that you are asked. Keep it brief and precise. No matter what is said, don't raise your voice, and keep your eyes on me. Your husband has the potential for making a good living from his law practice and his income from the Air Force Reserves. You have a rightful share of his income - that's the law. You are working at part-time, minimum wage jobs. You intend to go back to school so you can teach in the public schools, but God forbid, this might not happen. You have no place to live other than the apartment that you can barely pay for, and you have an old car, no insurance, and no money. Your assets consist of some jewelry that your parents gave you and some household items. Right?"

"Yes," I nodded, "but don't forget the $20,000 that we inherited from my mother. We used that to build a new kitchen and other things in our first home, the sale of which contributed mightily to our second home, and this house is in such bad shape that it would never sell."

"And you want this house?"

"Yes. It's a great lot in a great neighborhood, and it'll appreciate."

"You don't make life easy for yourself, do you?" he said as he handed me my jacket.

"I can't afford to yet," I replied.

Sonia

He had almost closed the door when the phone rang. "Better check."

He sank down into his seat. "What? Oh, for Christ's sake!" He put the receiver on his desk and rubbed his temples. "Your husband is having chest pains."

"Oh no," I said with real concern.

With receiver in hand, J. said, "Hell no, Max (long pause). Oh, shit, Your husband is pacing the floor and can't go into the court room," he said, loudly enough so that I could hear. They continued to talk, but I couldn't hear the words.

"Well, what do you want?"

"You know what I want and what I need. Aren't we going before a judge?"

"No," he said in an angry voice. "Tell me what you want!"

I was now afraid that they were manipulating me unfairly. In a tearful voice, I said, "I want custody of my youngest son, a place to live, a car, and some money."

"He won't give you custody of your son because he says you can't afford it. She says she wants the house (pause), says it's hardly livable. Essentially $30,000 went into it from her mother, for God's sake. On a $75,000 house? Get real!" Looking directly at me, he said, "He'll give it to you with a $20,000 lien, with a payment due when it's sold." I shook my head in disbelief. "She'll take it. Oh, she can have her jewelry, good, since none of it came from him. She has a part-time, minimum wage job and no money." There was a pause, and then he said, "He'll give you $900 for two months. Have they called an ambulance for your client yet? You better do that. And have you called the judge's chambers?"

To me, my lawyer said, "That's that. You'll get your divorce papers in the mail." He did not look as if he had won a victory. I was speechless and left without a word to find my friend, Barbara.

I felt weak and numb as I met Barbara. "Let's go to my house and have some coffee," she volunteered.

Over coffee, I told Barbara, "He manipulated me for the last time."

"How?" she looked worried.

"Going before the judge was cancelled, and a settlement was made over the phone by the four of us in about ten minutes."

"You didn't agree to this, did you?"

"Well, as we were on our way to court, a phone call informed us that my former husband was having chest pains and couldn't appear in court."

"Was an ambulance called?"

"Apparently not."

"What is the settlement?" I told her the details, as she shook her head in disbelief.

"I know........ but I'm free of him. I'll earn what I need. You must know how much this means to me."

"Well, you're on your own. That's for sure."

"I can live and be free and healthy, and I can give up all of that terrible guilt."

"Sure, if you don't work yourself to death."

Sonia

"Anything will be better than the stink of stale beer, sneaking around, and blaming each other for things that weren't in our control. I'm through with the pitiful, sad looks of apology and defeat."

"You are one determined woman, I'll say that."

"Now I'm free to plan the best future I can and take responsibility for it," I said in a quavering voice. "Having this thing finished will be a relief to my children, too, I think. I'll never really know what they think about it all, but I pray that they see their mother become a stable, productive human being again. They may even respect me a little someday."

"So at age fifty, you're going to make your mark in the world."

"Why not?"

"You really ARE relieved."

"Oh, yes. He can drive his new Cadillac, wear his Brooks Brother's clothes, and romance who he likes and be open about it, even respectable. None of this will be part of my life again. I am free!" I said, as I stood sobbing.

7. Back on Track

Graduate School

Although the campus was small, I was already lost, having asked for directions to the administration building for the third time. As I entered the Dean's office, I felt panicked - so much depended on the outcome of this visit. He was a tall, slim man with dyed hair. He introduced himself in a melodious voice. He probably sang in a choir, I thought. As he asked me to sit, he eased his long legs into a chair behind his desk.

"So you're interested in an advanced degree in education."

"Yes. I would like to return to teaching, but there are few vacancies in the classroom now. Is there a current need that is not being met?"

"Our primary need today is in Special Education. In fact, we have two grants available that pay for tuition and books. Would you like to take this manual home to review? It outlines the program in detail. If you are interested and qualify, the course begins in two weeks. The program does require a commitment to teach Special

Sonia

Education in this state for at least five years. Has your undergraduate transcript been mailed to me, as well as the evaluations of your former principals?"

"Yes," I said, as my hopes soared. A grant! How fortunate, I thought, as he ended the interview with a handshake and a smile. A thought raced through my mind with sickening speed. Would he even consider me if he knew that I had lived in the infamous Women's Building at Central State Hospital? That is history, I told myself sternly. Remember Omar!

My classes began two weeks later. I had been able to find used books at the campus bookstore. Ole Blue was working well, but a new concern surfaced - I would be spending a lot more money on gas, going back and forth ten miles. I would need more money. The next day, I went to the personnel department of a local department store and asked for part-time work. If I worked as a substitute teacher at least four or five days a week, attended night school three nights a week from six to nine on Mondays, Wednesdays, and Fridays, that left two nights and some Saturdays free, I could work those hours at the store.

Lady Luck was with me again. Someone was needed in the drapery department Tuesday and Thursday evenings and alternating Saturdays. I knew nothing about draperies and all of their apparatus, but I would learn, I told myself with false confidence. During school the next day, my mind wandered to my plans for that evening. Tonight would be my first class at the university. The course was called "The Remediation Of Learning Disabilities." It sounded big. After a quick shower with nice soap and a fluffy, clean, fresh, towel

(I no longer took this simple and common act for granted), I stood before my paltry wardrobe. What would I wear? I certainly wasn't a college girl. Neat and clean was the best that I could do. Pride couldn't be a factor at this stage of my life. I settled on a navy cotton skirt and a white shirt that reminded me of the school uniform I wore for ten years, the one that I had sworn that I'd never wear again. My brown shoes were worn down, but they'd get me there, I thought, as I stuffed things in my purse. I got a slight high as I put in my car keys, apartment key, driver's license, and some money. This was monumental in comparison to a year ago. I'd eat my sandwich on the way there.

As I neared the classroom, my heartbeat roared in my ears. The students were the same age as my children. I was so glad my children couldn't see me here.

My clothes were wrong, my hair was too long. I had seen two girls look at me and giggle. Were they wondering if I was the professor? A student? More likely, I was probably a lost janitor. At last, I found the right classroom. It was almost full of young vivacious girls, their sorority pins shining on their breasts. There was an empty chair near the back that I gratefully slipped into and waited. The two girls that I had seen earlier sat in front of me. They were talking about a dance they had attended with great animation.

A thought crossed my mind for the hundredth time. How can I compete with these young people? Just that brief thought made me break out into a cold sweat. From somewhere deep in my mind came the answer, "Why not? You'll be alright," I told myself.

I liked my professor. She was intelligent, mature, and dedicated to the difficult course that she was teaching. She demanded excellence in our projects and frequent tests. Her workshops with disabled students were excellent.

At first, the other students looked at me with curiosity, but in time, we spoke to each other briefly. There was another older woman in the class, and we became friends during the next two and half years while we were attending those classes.

Sometimes I wondered what my classmates would think if they knew my story up to that time. I walked slowly and carefully, trying to avoid any collisions with furniture or people. Daily, I prayed that my anticonvulsant would continue to serve me well. My friends in Al-Anon cheered me on. I still needed them and found time to go to a Saturday meeting.

The weeks went by slowly, as there were so many adjustments to make. The full schedule gave me purpose and direction. A new concern developed - the dangers of leaving the department store for the parking lot after 10 P.M. Eventually, another woman and I parked next to each other and left the building at the same time. I began carrying a whistle. I had become a fearful person, which annoyed me, yet my small salary checks and discounts were very valuable and eased the cash flow. Life was not easy, but it was good. There were many times I thought about asking my children to join me for a meal, but I had neither the time nor the money for that luxury yet.

I studied at the university library on Sundays and some Saturdays. I had learned to review course work for brief periods of time almost daily. I was sad not to see my children more often, but why should they come to see me? I had left them again and again. I'm sure there were other reasons, too; I had hardly been an admirable mother. All of my energy was channeled into my school work and surviving.

Will came back to my apartment once with our precious old dog, Hess. "He's not well and I can't care for him any longer, so it's up to you," he said. Our old friend of fourteen years became my roommate. We managed for almost a year. When I was gone for the entire day, I left him in the bathroom with the door gated. His problems increased, and the vet confirmed his suspicions of cancer. My heart almost broke as I agreed to putting our darling friend to sleep. We had loved each other for a long time.

School was demanding, but I was doing well. My poor rattled brain was in tune again. Indeed, my grades were considerably better than in my undergraduate days, when studying had to compete with social priorities. To this day, I have some flattering recommendations received from several professors during those difficult years.

It was with great pride that I sent my father an invitation to my graduation and a reception for the parents of the students who had graduated with honors. He was delighted, but since he was in his eighties and blind, he could not attend. I went by myself and celebrated with my newfound friends. I asked someone to take my picture with my camera, looking like a parent in an old navy blue skirt and a crisp white shirt - the same clothes that I had worn on my first day of class. It seemed appropriate.

St. Anne's

During April, I went downtown to the Catholic School Administration Center, hoping that there would be a vacancy for the fall term. I still had over a year of night school to complete before being awarded my master's degree.

A large and soulful woman named Catherine answered my questions. "I don't know of anything available now. Leave your name and phone number. Oh, you might as well fill out this form."

Catherine called ten days later as I was pouring over the classifieds, yellow marker in hand.

"If you are still interested, you can come down for an interview on Thursday at 11:00."

"I'll be there," I said with enthusiasm.

The interview went well. A teacher was needed for Middle School Language Arts. There would be thirty students daily, with ten each in grades six, seven, and eight. The sixth grade also needed a homeroom teacher who would also teach them social studies.

"Have you ever been the minority in an entire student body?"

"No," I replied softly.

She went on to say, "This school, St. Anne's, is near the center of the city and in a very rough neighborhood. There is considerable crime in this part of the city, and it can be dangerous."

My self-confident expression must have changed considerably. The section of the city that she was referring to was known to be a drug dealing pocket. I would never have dared to drive through it, even with the windows closed and the doors locked, much less get out of the car. Was I now contemplating working here? I would be arriving early in the morning and leaving late in the afternoon. There would be teachers' meetings after school and meetings with parents in the evening. My guardian angel would have to work overtime.

Sister interrupted my thoughts. "The salary is $800 a month. There are no benefits as of now, and we do not pay into your Social Security." My heart sank as I said, "I'll take the job."

"Good," she said enthusiastically. "You can pick up the Teacher's Editions for the courses you'll be teaching. I would like to see an overview of how you plan to teach these courses before summer vacation for my approval."

On my way home, I thought that the salary was sufficient to cover my mortgage of $500 for what was now my home. However, it was not enough to live on; I would still need the second job. My father had offered help, and I had promised to let him know if I had an emergency. Short of that, I told him it was up to me to work things out.

On the following day, I called my son, Tom. "Tom, I have a new job. Would you help me find the building?"

"Sure," he said good-naturedly. As we started down into the city, he looked concerned. "Why are we going so far south?"

I couldn't control a small sob, which ended up sounding like I was clearing my throat. "This is where I 'm going to be working, dear. This is the best I can do now, so wish me well."

"What I think we should do is find some alternate routes in and out of here, and then you can practice."

Sonia

How I loved him for suggesting that and caring.

The principal was short and rotund, with a pretty round face, light blue eyes, and short, curly gray hair. Her burgundy polyester pant suit was bursting at the seams. We discussed my lesson plans for the year and she approved them with some suggestions. I had taught the sixth grade in Delaware for a year, but I had never had an African-American student in any of my classrooms, not even when I was near the military base. The children weren't the challenge; the neighborhood was.

On the blackboard in my English class, I wrote in bold letters:

THE ENGLISH LANGUAGE IS OUR MOST PRECIOUS TOOL.

USE IT WITH PRECISION.

There were groans and protests as creative writings were written, corrected, and rewritten again. The children learned to spell, read the classics, and above all, they learned to express themselves with more confidence and precision.

One fall day, we received a notice that there would be a writing contest for all twelve of the Catholic schools in the city. The subject was to write an original prayer of Thanksgiving. When I told the classes that we were going to participate, their protests surprised me.

"They won't pick us," one said.

"We never get picked," another person chimed in.

"Some honkey up north will win, in their lilly-white schools."

The Moving Finger

"Well, well," I murmured, "we'll see. Your English assignment tonight will be to make a list of five things that you are grateful for, and then write a short paragraph about each one of these things. We'll look these over tomorrow. Remember, the first prize will be taking your parents to the Governor's mansion for breakfast with the Governor, a trophy, and a small amount of money."

We had two weeks left before sending our entries. The children wrote their drafts and corrected those of their classmates, and then we voted for the three that we would submit from our English classes.

Weeks went by and we had almost forgotten about the contest until one day Sister Ann Marie came into the eighth grade class with a wide smile. "I have good news! Someone at St Ann's has won the writing contest."

"In this school?" someone called out.

"No, from all the schools that entered," her round face beamed.

Donna, a bright and ambitious girl, had won. She had agonized over her work. The newspaper photographer took good pictures of her and her parents, who beamed with pride. Donna held her trophy high. She planned to keep the twenty-five dollars for something special. A certain pride developed in our elite group.

At a later date, there was a similar contest with public speaking. The assignment was to present an idea or object and then sell it to the audience. We practiced on the stage in front of younger children and then the faculty. We chose a tall and poised young man who commanded respect. There were only six participants that night. St. Anne's brought home another trophy - Larry won third place and brought back the ribbon for all of us to "glory over."

Black History Month in February was rich in things to study, read, and write about. We wrote poetry and learned some techniques for doing research. Kwanzaa was met with varying degrees of interest by the families, but it was explored.

The time that I spent at St Anne's are very special to me. I would regret not having that experience. Those years were rich in experience and growth. I still smile when I think of the first day there, when everyone seemed to look alike to me. In time, I became much more perceptive and understanding.

There were no "problem children" at St Anne's. Most of the students were from the second or third generation in their families to go there. The fact that they were there testified to their parents' interest and concern with their education and well-being. Most of the children lived within walking distance and were accompanied to school by family members or friends.

On the second day of school, a fourth grade boy approached me and asked, "Is that dark blue car yours?" I nodded yes.

"Well, I'm going home after school for a gun to shoot out all your tires."

In my no-nonsense voice, I replied, "You do that and I'll tell your mother, and you'll have to go to the public school." There was a slight smile on his lips as he walked away.

One school day per week, the students, faculty, and a surprising number of adults attended Mass. Although Catholics are notorious for lack of enthusiasm for singing in church, the singing at

The Moving Finger

St. Anne's on those days was remarkably good. When the hymns were quiet and soft, I could feel the Holy Spirit ascend over us. The young children's voices had almost a mewing tone at times that has never left me. When the tempo was fast, the hymns rang out with joy and enthusiasm or sadness and despair.

During the middle of my third year at St. Anne's, I had a phone call from the public school's personnel office. A rather strident voice said, "We have been told that you were a recipient of the grant for the teaching of Special Education in the public schools."

"Yes, I finished my studies a short time ago."

"We have a position open now. How soon can you start?"

"I have another semester to complete at the private school where I am teaching."

The voice said rather strictly, "Perhaps I misunderstood, but I believe that you signed a contract to teach Special Education in the public schools when you were needed."

The next day I repeated this conversation to Sister Ann Marie. "We will hate to lose you, but oddly enough, a former teacher from here has told us that she wants to come back. She could finish the semester for you."

I left St. Anne's with sadness, but my memories are rich. The song "We Will Overcome" as I stood with my students, singing loudly with them in anticipation of their future, still resounds in my ears.

Public Schools

After St. Anne's, I was assigned to a school where I would complete the semester for a teacher that had a medical emergency. I would put into practice my new endorsements that I had just received from the university that supposedly qualified me to teach the learning disabled, emotionally disturbed, and neurologically challenged. It did not prepare me for the hostility that my groups of children met from other teachers, parents, and sometimes principals. Indeed, the principal did not want special education in his school. These groups of children did present unique challenges for schools. School grade averages and test results were reduced by these children's lower scores. They created added disruptions in the halls and playground. The office was required by law to meet the added calls and paperwork as well as to provide support to the people who advised and monitored the Special Education groups. Each child had an I.E.P. (Individual Educational Program) which clearly spelled out the goals for the semester in each academic subject, behavior, and any other specified need. This I.E.P. was signed by the parent, teacher, principal, and any other individual involved (such as the speech therapist or physical therapist.) It was not easy, but I enjoyed it for the next five years, seeing both successes and failures among my students and their families.

I will never forget the time that my students, who varied in age from eight to ten, and I were watching the blast-off of the ill-fated space shuttle that contained several astronauts, including a young teacher. When I saw the shuttle disintegrate, tears of horror welled in my eyes, but several students began to laugh - apparently lacking any sense of the reality of the situation or empathy. I bit my tongue to keep from reacting strongly to their behavior. Their regular teacher recovered and returned the next semester.

My next assignment was further away from my home and located in a poor inner-city neighborhood. There were almost equal numbers of black and white children in the school and in my classes. The vast majority of the students were from poor families, but the attitudes of their parents varied widely. Some were irresponsible and unmotivated, while others were very involved in their children's welfare and expected them to be taught well and to learn. Of course, there were those who failed to meet their children's most basic needs. One of these students of mine was named Mary Scott.

It was a regal name, and it piqued my interest. My "learning disabled" class was large that year - seven boys and five girls, with ages ranging from nine to thirteen. The school bell rang, and I left my post at the door: Eleven of the children had arrived and the last one was coming down the hall with her registration card in hand. So this is Mary Scott, I thought. She was a tall and thin girl with beautiful posture, a long neck that held her head gracefully, warm and clear dark brown skin, and a graceful pace that approached a glide. Little did I know how much this child would come to mean to me.

My first day's routine unfolded. First, there had to be silence and order. To my students' evident surprise, I gave no loud orders to sit down and be quiet. Instead, I walked to the blackboard and wrote in bold letters, SIT DOWN PLEASE. No one could read the words, but I had their attention. Then, mouthing these words in a loud whisper, they encouraged each other to sit down.

Sonia

In my first report about Mary, I wrote: "Mary is very silent. Her eyes are nervous, and she avoids direct eye contact. She apparently has had very little success academically. Her records profile her as a non-reader and failing in all subjects."

Although Mary showed little interest in me, I was able to break the ice two weeks later. "My grandmother said only devils have blue eyes," she said boldly. Her large, slightly-slanted dark eyes were fixed on the floor. I encouraged her to sit down at eye level with me, and we looked steadily into each other's eyes. We both burst out laughing.

"What do you think?" I asked in a silly voice.

With sincerity, she answered, "I don't know yet."

As time passed, I became concerned about Mary, who looked exhausted when she came to school. There were days when her skin had a gray cast. I would make a home visit. Her mother ignored my requests to visit school. Academically, Mary was making progress and was proud of it. Her eyes glistened with happiness as her word recognition improved steadily. I was encouraged to see a learning barrier slowly dissipating, but she appeared to need more encouragement at home.

I decided to go to her home to speak to her mother. She lived in a "project" nearby. Her building had a bad reputation for drug dealing, and there was a shooting at least twice a week. Mary's mother looked angry as she partially opened her door.

"What do you want?"

"I'm Mary's teacher and would like to talk to you."

"Well, talk."

The Moving Finger

"May I come in?"

She slowly opened the door just wide enough for me to sidle in.

Two toddlers were sleeping in a playpen. A huge man about thirty was draped over a chair. He came to his feet slowly. The three of us talked about Mary's needs.

Six months later, I was called to the office telephone. It was Mary and she was almost hysterical.

"Miz Hudson?"

"Yes, Mary. What's wrong?"

"Miz Hudson, I've walked all night and can't get rid of it."

"Get rid of what?" I asked, almost annoyed.

"Momma used a coat hanger last night. I'm bleeding, but it didn't come out."

"Oh my God," flashed across my mind, and every muscle in my body tensed with emotion.

"Mary, who is with you?"

"Momma, but she's asleep."

"Someone will be there to help you in a few minutes. Can you let them in?"

"Yes, but not the police."

"Someone will be there. Go lie down and put your feet up."

Thank God Jerry, the social worker, was there that morning. He was driven to the house by a policeman, and Mary was taken to the emergency room.

I never saw Mary Scott again. She and her mother moved and left no forwarding address. Jerry and I talked about the case, and I wondered what could have been done. I tried to talk through the tears, mumbling, "This is not fair. What will happen to her?" In my heart, I knew that the thin and tall young girl with an I.Q. of 50 and no one to protect her probably wouldn't make it.

I still feel anger and worry about the young girl with the lovely name of Mary Scott.

8. A New Life

Paul and I

As I look back, it seems as if Paul and I were destined to meet. This man came into my life during my early fifties. I was secure now and had a good teaching job. My income was paying the bills with a little left over. Having continuity in my work and the insurance perks that went with the job, I finally had direction and self-confidence. My health had also improved greatly.

It was during this time that my friend Sarah invited me to a party that she was hosting. Our former husbands had become friends in law school and at Air Force Reserve meetings, and they had become drinking buddies. Over the years, Sarah had developed a curious and quick intellect. If she had lived in Paris in the days of Josephine Bonaparte, she would have had a thriving and popular salon. I can visualize her stimulating and coaxing her guests to discuss important issues. We are sorority sisters, as we are both members of Kappa Alpha Theta from Indiana University, although she is younger than I am.

Sonia

Sarah had become restless and decided to take some secretarial courses. The lovely and witty invitation came in January. Sarah's calligraphy was studied, unique, and impressive. The purpose of the party was to introduce her new boss, Paul. I had seen a picture of him in the newspaper, in which he was being introduced as the Vice-President of a "Think Tank" from New York. I had never heard of a "Think Tank." He had come to Indianapolis from Washington, D. C., where he had worked for the C.I.A. for thirty years. I had lived in Washington for a year and had loved it. This would be an interesting party.

Sarah's large and lovely home was used often for entertaining friends and acquaintances. As I looked around the room, I saw some old friends. Shirley had taken a new job at Lilly. Ruth stood tall and gracefully posed by the fireplace. Her cool good looks were appealing. Sarah had invited several single women and three couples. Where was the guest of honor? I wondered.

Eventually, he was paraded around the room with clever introductions. He was about sixty, and he was tall and trim. His gray hair, a mass of curls and waves, gave him a special air of sophistication. As we were introduced, we gave each other a quick appraising look as Sarah quipped, "Sonia is the person who lived in D.C."

"Is that so?" he said politely, as they walked away. Paul sat across the table from me, and he sat next to Shirley. They were having a lively conversation. I was seated next to Dan, someone I had known from law school days. Our conversation was easy and relaxed. I would have been a boring tablemate for Paul, I thought to myself. I wondered if Sarah and Paul would have a future together.

Paul called two weeks later and asked me to dinner, an event that became increasingly common. During the next two years, common interests and ties became evident, and our dates, which regularly covered weekends and sometimes more, developed an easy and exciting rhythm.

Paul's father, an American citizen of Belgian ancestry, had brought his new French bride to Madison, Wisconsin, where they lived near my grandmother's house on Lake Mendota. I had walked across that area many times as a young child looking for beach treasures. Our fathers both taught at Wisconsin, although not at the same time. A cousin of Paul's father had lived in the Fifth Avenue apartment house that was owned by Frank Matchette, my father's uncle. Her husband had advised Frank to sell 820 Fifth Avenue, the apartment building across the street, in 1929, just before the start of the Great Depression. This was a lot of shared history.

We had many common tastes and interests. We both enjoyed good literature, music, food, and especially dancing. I think dancing together well and with great enthusiasm is what encouraged us to see each other regularly.

When we went to the opera, a symphony, or a movie, we seemed to lean toward each other in our seats, and we were usually touching. After a while, we automatically went hand-in-hand. We liked to be connected. I saw a tear fall several times during an emotional event, and I began to love his sensitive side.

I told Paul about my bouts with depression and hospitalizations. He was interested and sympathetic, but not judgmental. We were both divorced Catholics and wondered about our future roles in the church.

During the second year of our friendship, we met each other's remaining parents and children. Paul's son, Charles, is younger than my sons.

We were married two years later in a simple home ceremony. The husband of my dear friend, Barbara, married us. Our children, Paul's mother, and cousin Odette, along with several friends, were in attendance. A delayed honeymoon in Paris where Paul was born was the beginning of many happy years and foreign trips together.

We took a safari in Africa, listening in awe to the night noises and the occasional padding of feet past our tent, followed by the lights of our guides. In China, we walked the Great Wall and were fascinated by the extraordinary activity and energy all around us. A Yale tour (Paul's Alma Mater) took us to Greece and the Greek Islands in luxury. We decided that we could live happily on the island of Santorini. Our trips to France, especially Paris, have given us happy memories.

We both retired and enjoyed a year of living in Old Town in Alexandria, Virginia. Presently, we live in a condominium on Sarasota Bay, Florida.. We love each other. We appreciate our good fortune in meeting each other, and we expect to remain together for the rest of our lives.

It didn't enter my mind that there could be another man in my life. During those awful years of fear and deprivation, that seemed inconceivable. Paul has helped me once again to become excited about life. The romance and love that we found as mature people is enviable. We have shared almost twenty years in trust and harmony. Caring for our elderly parents together has brought us even closer. As we watched our children mature and find their places in the world, we shared their successes. Three weddings and three grandchildren have contributed to our happiness.

We look forward to the experiences of the last chapters of our lives together. I am so thankful that we were given this second chance.

Poems

DEAR SONIA

This was a year we settled down.
No game safari or Chinese town,
No Cretan ruins or Parthenon,
No boxes for our antique vases
Or fitting squares in oval spaces.

On winter days we feast our eyes
With soaring birds in azure skies
With leaping fish 'neath crimson clouds,
While friendships grows in wider circles
And Sam, like us, feels right at home.

Sonia

In summer house, through tall pines seen,
Walloon Lake glistens in the breeze,
Which brings the freshness of the North,
While we perform our social duty
By giving a Titanic party.

And all the children made us proud
As John's and Laura's marriage vows
of another generation,
While Charles achieved his graduation.

Most important, our relations
Are building on their firm foundations.
For we are ever growing closer,
And you will be forever,
My greatest love.
    Merry Christmas,
    Paul

DEAR PAUL
Sarah, my friend, to me did send
A true love.
I liked his style and after a while
Became his wife.

We've shared a lot over fifteen years,

The Moving Finger

Laughed, loved, even shed some tears.
We've traveled over foreign lands,
Usually going hand-in-hand.

Your steady base and foundation
Light and fuel my adulation.
A good team we do make,
From us, our sons lessons take.

We are quick to have reactions
Not always to our satisfaction.
Storms do brew over being right,
But after the storm, there's always light.

After all is said and done,
I'm so glad you're the one
With whom I share my life.
Your ever loving, docile, wife,
    SONIA

9. Reflections

A MEETING WITH WILL

As my book neared completion - at the final sign-off stage for the galley - one section, *The Cuban Crisis*, troubled me. I simply don't remember much of what happened in the fall and early winter 1962, except for some brief, but strong impressions of what for me were dramatic events. Although I have tried to piece together a more or less coherent broader picture from what others have told me, I was concerned that this picture might be inaccurate and misleading.

We had left the safety of our beloved university campus for a military base. Will was in his last year of Law School and I was in the seventh month of a sensitive pregnancy. I can't explain why my memory closed down with this move, but it did.

My exceedingly generous parents knew the facts, but they are deceased. Will's very caring and selfless mother was there, but she is in a nursing home and months away from her one hundredth birthday. The children were either too young or unborn. The only other living witness is my former husband, Will.

After much thought I decided to contact Will. The next day, after an unsatisfactory telephone conversation, I wrote him a letter in which I spelled out what I could and could not remember about the events in that period - one that became so critical to our lives. I suggested that we meet at his rented house, north of Naples, Florida, where he and his present wife were spending some time, in the hope that he could help fill some of the blanks in my memory. He agreed, and we had a couple of hours of friendly conversation.

During that time, I learned enough from him to considerably rewrite the *Cuban Crisis* section of my book so as to make it more accurate. Perhaps also our meeting helped us to achieve a more satisfactory closure to what had been a complex, stressed, and turbulent, but loving relationship.

He gave me some background on the Cuban Crisis and on his military role. He filled large gaps in my memory and corrected my misconceptions about our move to Columbus, our stay there, and my parents' arrival. He told me things about myself that I did not remember. But about some things he remembered little.

Will answered the door leaning on his walker. Parkinson's disease was ravaging him.

His hands trembled and his feet shuffled as he led me to a chair in the den. We had given each other a light embrace and a buzz on the cheek. After exchanging pleasantries he began with his memories of 1962.

Sonia

"I had been attending a Unit Training Assembly at the Air Force base in Columbus for the weekend and had decided to make the forty five minute drive to Bloomington to spend Saturday night with you and the children. At midnight there was a phone call from the base telling me to report to the base at six that morning for an active duty commitment for up to one year. The "Cuban Crisis" was under way. Military only: no provisions for dependants at this time. That morning I called my mother and asked her to help you with the children for a few days and I reported to the base for Active Duty.

By noon that Sunday half of the C 19's (also called "flying boxcars") were dispatched to Fort Campbell, Kentucky, where they picked up the 101st Airborne . They then went to McCoy Air Force base in Orlando, Florida, where they sat for three days. I had been assigned to the Command Post in Columbus. Among my jobs was Flight Instructor, which involved giving flight checks at night. After a week I rented an apartment near the base and came for you and the children. At that point we lost access to university housing for some time."

"This move upset you a great deal and you began to cry a lot. The uncertain conditions frightened you. Your parents came to Columbus, which helped in many ways. We even had a decent Christmas together, tree and all. What else do you want to know?"

"Will", I asked timidly, "What was the matter with me? What was holding me back? "

He lowered his eyes. " I don't know, I'm not a doctor. I asked your doctor the same question. There was never a real answer."

"How was my mental / physical health when we left Bloomington?"

"You were doing quite well in Bloomington. You had begun a routine and had built a network of friends that was very helpful in job sharing and a social life with other young mothers nearby."

I can remember some of these friends happily.

"Did I do much in the apartment, like cook or clean?"

" It varied a lot."

" How did this pregnancy go compared to the others?"

" It went pretty well, there was no real problem. Dr. Frank took good care of you. We didn't leave you alone."

"Why ?" I asked.

"You were having seizures."

"Very many?' I whispered through clenched teeth.

"It varied a lot".

With a sweeping gesture of my hand toward the floor I asked: "Was I writhing on the floor? Did I fall down or slump over?" My heart was racing, awaiting an answer.

"No, but I had to put something in your mouth so you wouldn't bite your tongue."

"Was it that bad?" I asked, shocked. How awful for him I sobbed inside.

"Let's not go there anymore", he said, "this was a long time ago".

I shook my head up and down in agreement. What is so strange is that I have been seizure free for over twenty five years. After in-depth testing by a neurologist over twenty years ago I was told that I was now no more of a candidate for seizures than the ordinary man on the street.

"I don't know, you were so fearful, so angry about what had happened to us," he said.

"Maybe there was scar tissue from the surgery."

"Who took me to the hospital for John's birth?"

"I don't know, I really don't." Presumably, Will was on special duty that night.

"You didn't like the doctor who delivered John, did you?"

"Neither of us did. He seemed uneasy with your case. He thought he was entitled to payment for your entire prenatal and postnatal care even though he saw you only once or twice before your delivery."

"How was John taken to Riley hospital?"

"I don't know," he replied.

"Don't you remember", I said in surprise. He had "Hyline Membrane's Disease" and needed a "rocking isolette" to clear his lungs of fluid.

"Hyline Membrane" rings a bell. I just don't remember anything else."

Reflecting later on this meeting, I wondered whether Will's lapses in memory were due to the medication he was taking for Parkinson's or to the trauma these painful events had inflicted.

As I left, I was saddened by Will's deteriorating condition. Yet his dark eyes sparkled with the same merriment as in his youth and his wonderful dimples still flashed as he made humorous remarks.

"I am glad to see you with Paul", he said. "I'd hate to see you alone."

"We're lucky to have had a second chance, aren't we?"

We parted with the same thought : of having done the best we knew how under very trying and difficult conditions.

Fear of Failure

It has been almost forty years since I was locked into the fear that consumed and controlled my life. The constant struggle to live as if nothing had happened to me since my neurosurgery and postpartum depression was futile and destructive. I felt that I had failed my young children as we went from one crisis to another. Despite my newly acquired limitations, I strove to meet unrealistic expectations, which were mainly my own, and to constantly prove that I was in control of my body and mind. Sharing my feelings with my husband and with sympathetic and compassionate female friends might have helped, but my husband was partly in denial, and my relationships with friends were not comfortable enough to discuss such intimate and sensitive matters. For example, I was not part of a neighborhood group that met for coffee or bridge and might have provided an easy entree to "girl talk."

What was it, then, that lifted the terrible cloud that hovered over me for so many years and the fears that possessed me? I don't think the "shock treatments" were of much value. I was terrified of them, and never did they give me any relief from my depression for more than a month or so. The pharmacological treatments were haphazard and sometimes experimental. "Psychosocial" treatment was essentially nonexistent.

I believe that my path to recovery began with the time I spent in Central State Hospital. That was the place where I began to regain some power over my life. It began in small steps: working eight hours a day in a highly regulated environment, having a small living space to care for, having a routine that didn't overwhelm me, and directing my energy toward others. I also learned to focus my energy on survival, on the present rather than the self-imposed obligations for the future.

Looking back at my recovery process, I believe that leaving my husband and living on my own were essential steps in regaining confidence and control over my life. I focused my efforts on making ends meet and using my abilities as best I could. Al-Anon, my adult children, and some good friends helped, but I had to rely mainly on my own efforts. I still have a low-grade depression that is managed very well by a low dose of antidepressant that has been developed in the past decade. Depression can be treated, so don't give up your search for answers! Treatments for mental illness are improving and future breakthroughs are possible.

Life has softened since I met Paul. I feel safe, treasured, and fortunate. It is only now that I have the will and desire to tell my story.

A Blanket

Dear Sons,

It was cold last night in Florida. The last few mornings have been unseasonably cool. This morning, as I pulled up my lovely, peach-colored duvet and snuggled down in warm comfort, I thought about another blanket that was valuable to me at one time - the time, almost forty years ago, when I lived in the Women's Building at Central State Hospital. There were five hundred women living there at the time. Some had been there for over thirty years. Some would remain there for the rest of their lives. There were those like me who were using experimental drugs for depression.

When fall arrived, the heat came on. A rank, sour smell permeated the building and everything in it, and the thought of it still turns my stomach. There were times when the ancient furnace didn't work properly, and it was either cold or almost unbearably hot.

My little metal bed was low to the floor and rusted. The stained mattress was thin and filled with a straw-like material. Our thin blankets were dark gray, stiff, and scratchy, and they had a variety of holes that were used as means of identification.

My blanket had many holes, and it was very important to me. It helped to keep me warm, and it gave me protection and a sense of well-being.

During my time at Central State Hospital, I had learned that there were ways of concealing small luxuries. I had accumulated several small bars of Ivory soap. Eventually, my blanket absorbed some of this clean, fresh fragrance. It was a luxury all my own.

I enjoy my beautiful peach-colored duvet and sheets, but my small, thin gray blanket with the holes and untold history gave me protection and a sense of well-being also. I remember it now with fondness and appreciation.

Love always,

Your MOM

Uncle Frank

Aunt Nell and Uncle Frank Matchette still play an important role in my life.

Sixty-five years after their deaths, I am reminded of them almost daily. Aunt Nell commisioned the portrait by an excellent artist of my twin brother and sister, which hangs in our living room. When we feel festive, we use their lovely table linens on the dining room table where the Matchettes ate their wedding breakfast. We use their china and sterling that was bought at Tiffany's. When glancing at Fifth Avenue real estate advertising in the New York Times, I think about the buildings on the corner of Fifth and 62nd Street (numbers 817 and 820) that were owned by Frank Matchette, where I spent many happy days during my childhood.

I was overwhelmed when my father agreed that I could take over as president of a foundation that Frank established in his will. It is a small foundation that funds lectures and seminars in philosophy. Paul and I work together on the Matchette Foundation's activities. We enjoy the intellectual challenge and the small checks that we receive monthly.

With pride, we tell of our most famous grant recipient of many years ago, a Catholic philosopher that was then named Cardinal Wojtila of Poland. He was awarded a grant to come to a conference in the United States. Today, he is Pope John Paul II.

My brother and I went to college with the inheritance that we received from Uncle Frank. I think of him and Aunt Nell with love and gratitude. They were childless, but they treated us like their own children in many ways.

My Dearest Sons,

As I read my "galley" for the last time before sending it to my publisher I am dismayed. "I" is the most commonly used word in the entire text. There may have been a more clever way of telling this accounting and having it less "I" dominated but, it's too late for that now.

Our burdens have been heavy on this path called life, especially yours. I will never know all the scars you carry from having me as your mother, during those early years. My greatest hope is that you have developed into empathetic, stable and resourceful men. I am grateful that you can witness both of your parents in stable and happy marriages.

When you are faced with life's trials look to tomorrow and focus on the future. You might even call to mind the poem of OMAR KHAYYAM .

Thank you for being my children.. Love

Always,

your,

MOTHER

Our home "Pinecrest" in Northern Michigan

#23 in front of "Pinecrest"

Their last sailing together on #23
Will, Willy and Sonia

Buildings 817 and 820
5th Ave. and 62nd St. New York City

A family dinner in 817's Penthouse 1929

Carrie and Sonia in France

Will in flight suit
Dover Del. on his way to Greenland

Our Family
Pretending that all is normal and happy

Sonia and her adult sons